Advance Praise

"This compelling book is an invitation to leap forward in our practices, policies, and perspectives related to students with disabilities. It calls us to adopt educational services and supports that are ambitious, effective, individualized, and always inclusive."

—**Erik W. Carter,** Cornelius Vanderbilt Professor of Special Education,
Vanderbilt University

"No, inclusion is not dead; rather, it has evolved. Wehmeyer and Kurth reframe inclusion away from classroom placement to a multi-tiered, school-wide approach emphasizing personalized, strengths-based, and effective instruction—so that, truly, all can achieve. For the first time in special education history, we now have the models and the technology to make inclusion become reality—and this book paves the way by setting new directions. A must-read for any educator who is committed to moving inclusive education forward."

—**Linda M. Bambara, Ed.D.,** Emeritus Professor of Special Education,
Lehigh University

"*Inclusive Education in a Strengths-Based Era* by Michael Wehmeyer and Jennifer Kurth provides a contemporary and very readable guide to what special education should look like and accomplish for persons with disabilities as we progress through the 21st century. Highlights of this work include the articulation of our changing understanding of special education's legal and legislative foundations; a description of the shift from a remedial to a support perspective; an emphasis on a strength-based approach to education; and a forthright acknowledgment that it is wrongful to exclude students from general education content and settings. I highly recommend this work."

—**Lewis Jackson, Ed.D.,** Emeritus Professor of Special Education,
University of Northern Colorado

INCLUSIVE EDUCATION
in a
STRENGTHS-BASED ERA

**The Norton Series on Inclusive Education
for Students with Disabilities**
Michael L. Wehmeyer and Jennifer A. Kurth, series editors

The Series on Inclusive Education for Students with Disabilities is a publishing home for books that offer strengths-based approaches to understanding disability and that propose educational supports to enable all students, with and without disabilities, to succeed. Books in the series provide practical, research-referenced information for educators who teach students with disabilities in typical education contexts with their non-disabled peers.

Inclusive Education in a Strengths-Based Era
Michael L. Wehmeyer and Jennifer A. Kurth

Norton Books in Education

INCLUSIVE EDUCATION
in a
STRENGTHS-BASED
ERA

Mapping the Future of the Field

MICHAEL L. WEHMEYER
JENNIFER A. KURTH

W. W. NORTON & COMPANY
Independent Publishers Since 1923

This work is intended as a general information resource for educators. It is not a substitute for appropriate professional education or training, peer review, or clinical supervision. Standards of clinical practice and protocol change over time, and no technique or recommendation is guaranteed to be safe or effective in all circumstances. For case-specific questions and guidance, please consult with your school and/or community mental-health clinicians.

Any URLs displayed in this book link or refer to websites that existed as of press time. The publisher is not responsible for, and should not be deemed to endorse or recommend, any website other than its own or any content not created by it. The author, also, is not responsible for any third-party material.

For information about permission to reproduce selections from this book, write to Permissions, W. W. Norton & Company, Inc., 500 Fifth Avenue, New York, NY 10110

For information about special discounts for bulk purchases, please contact W. W. Norton Special Sales at specialsales@wwnorton.com or 800-233-4830

Manufacturing by Versa Press
Book design by Carole Desnoes
Production manager: Katelyn MacKenzie

Library of Congress Cataloging-in-Publication Data

Names: Wehmeyer, Michael L., author. | Kurth, Jennifer A., author.
Title: Inclusive education in a strengths-based era : mapping the future of the field / Michael L. Wehmeyer and Jennifer A. Kurth.
Description: First edition. | New York : W.W. Norton & Company, 2021. | Series: Inclusive education for students with disabilities series |
Includes bibliographical references and index.
Identifiers: LCCN 2020054541 | ISBN 9781324015994 (paperback) | ISBN 9781324016007 (epub)
Subjects: LCSH: Inclusive education. | Children with mental disabilities—Education. | Learning disabled children—Education. | Individualized education programs.
Classification: LCC LC1200 .W43 2021 | DDC 371.9/046—dc23
LC record available at https://lccn.loc.gov/2020054541

W. W. Norton & Company, Inc., 500 Fifth Avenue, New York, N.Y. 10110
www.wwnorton.com

W. W. Norton & Company Ltd., 15 Carlisle Street, London W1D 3BS

1 2 3 4 5 6 7 8 9 0

This book is dedicated to the many teachers and administrators whose efforts demonstrate the effectiveness and importance of inclusive and personalized education.

Contents

Acknowledgments

The authors would like to acknowledge and thank our editor, Carol Collins, and her colleagues at Norton Professional Books for the opportunity to edit the Norton Series on Inclusive Education and Students with Disabilities. We are excited by the chance to work with authors who are creating a "fourth generation" of inclusive practices and fortunate to work with the exceptional professionals at Norton Books in Education.

Introduction

Educational practices exist within contexts, whether that context is set by federal legislation like the Every Student Succeeds Act or the Individuals With Disabilities Education Act, or involve social and civil contexts such as what we (in the U.S.) experienced in 2020 due to the COVID pandemic and the movement toward social justice, or as a result of economic or environmental circumstances such as those created by the global economy. In *Endrew F. v. Douglas County School District* (2018), the U.S. Supreme Court held that an appropriate public education, as guaranteed by federal law, is one in which each student has an appropriately ambitious educational program that gives them the chance to meet challenging objectives, and that the student's educational program must be determined only after careful consideration of the child's individual potential for growth. We believe that this ruling creates a new and powerful context in which to make greater strides in ensuring that every student receives a high quality education.

The Endrew decision is not the only contextual factor that is dramatically changing the landscape for the education of all learners, including students with disabilities. Before the worldwide global pandemic, there was already a movement toward more personalized learning. For good or ill, the pandemic seems to have accelerated the role of technology in education and, we believe, will ultimately result in schools' adoption of personalized, self-determined learning. We say that with some certainty because, as we discuss in this book, the world today is very different from the world 100 and 50 years ago, when the current education system and special education system (respectively) were established. We believe that these global changes and the drive toward personalized education and self-determined learning provide opportunities to create a "fourth generation of inclusive practices" that are predicated on what Endrew declared: all children deserve the opportunity to have a challenging education based upon student strengths and potential for growth. There is a unique opportunity to jettison separate, siloed systems that have been intractable with regard to achieving the vision of full inclusion. Further, the contexts in which disability itself is understood are changing dramatically. We are, for the first time in history, poised to approach the design of educational supports within a strengths-based paradigm. Strengths-based approaches are based on social models of disability: on the assumption that understandings of disability are rooted in the attitudes, structures, and environments in society and the restrictions inherent in these contexts. Within such models and approaches, disability is viewed as a part of, and not apart from, typical human experiences. Adopting the supports paradigm driven by strengths-based approaches to disability empowers educators to abandon long-held presumptions about limitations and deficits and to design supports that enable all learners to succeed.

The role of educators will, inevitably, change in a context in which education adopts strengths-based approaches that are personalized, emphasize self-determined learning, and provide supports that enable student success in typical contexts with their non-disabled peers. But, we believe that these changes provide opportunities for special educators to impact positive outcomes for more students, to provide expertise and experience that contributes to the success of the whole school, and ultimately enables them to achieve the goals that drove them to become an educator in the first place.

Books in our series provide theory-to-practice bridges for inclusive practices; that is, they provide practitioner-friendly, research-referenced information for educators who teach students with disabilities in typical education contexts with their non-disabled peers. The focus of volumes in the series is on emerging and innovative educational practice directions that have direct implications for building systems of support that enhance the inclusion of students with disabilities in schools. In development are books on implementing a supports paradigm in education, differentiating instruction, providing schoolwide supports, and team teaching and collaboration. Under discussion are books on self-determined learning, teaching core content subjects in inclusive settings, assessment to promote inclusive education, and the role of technology and universal design in promoting inclusive practices. The purpose of this volume is to lay the foundation for future volumes that provide that information. Our intent is to describe in full the contexts that are impacting the education of all learners, to identify the intent of federal legislation like IDEA and court rulings like Endrew, and to provide a broad overview of how we, as educators, move forward to support and enable all students to become self-determined learners and to succeed in the changing context of education in a post-COVID world.

About the Authors

Michael Wehmeyer has been engaged in educating learners with exceptional support needs for more than forty years, serving as a special education teacher, an advocate, a researcher, and a teacher-trainer. His work is focused on promoting self-determination and inclusive practices and believes that the ideas in this book provide a road map to a future in which all students receive an education that enables them to live full, rich lives in their communities.

Jennifer Kurth has been a teacher and teacher educator for over twenty years. She also researches methods of implementing high-quality inclusive education, and is optimistic about a future in which all students are highly valued members of their schools and communities.

INCLUSIVE EDUCATION
in a
STRENGTHS-BASED
ERA

What Is Special Education Today?

Inclusive and Personalized Education

One refrain heard frequently in discussions of 21st-century learning is that the current education system was built for a bygone era; that it was built for "an economy and a society that no longer exists (National Education Association, 2016, p. 5). In the current global economic context, students can no longer be successful focusing only on core academic skills, they must learn how to communicate, to be creative, to engage in critical thinking, to solve problems, and to self-determine learning.

What one hears less frequently are discussions about these issues as they pertain to the education of learners with disabilities. After all, what is now titled the 2004 Individuals With Disabilities Education Act (IDEA) is approaching its 50th anniversary. It seems obvious that the context in which IDEA was written and has been implemented is no longer the context in which students with disabilities are educated and that the demands for postschool life today are very different from those half a century ago. Indeed, one can even suggest that the students who are educated under IDEA are different from the students for whom the law was originally written, or that how we understand disability has changed in the past 50 years.

It is, in our estimation, worth asking ourselves what, exactly, special education is today. Who do we teach now, and what and where should we be teaching them? Of course, the baseline answer to the "who do we teach" question is that, as special educators, we teach students who, by virtue of meeting criteria set by IDEA, are eligible to receive special education services.

But that seems to be an entirely unsatisfactory answer considering the rapid and systemic changes in education today. Perhaps this worked fine in an era of self-contained settings (although we would contend that it did not), but how does it work as we shift to an era of schoolwide applications, educating increasingly more learners in general education settings? Two of the presumptions in multitiered systems of supports (which we discuss in depth in Chapter 2) are that all students receive high-quality instruction in typical education settings and that, for students who have difficulty mastering content, what changes is the intensity, type, or quality of the instruction, rather than removing the student from the classroom to receive "special education" somewhere else. Logically, it seems to us, the special educator's role within inclusive classrooms and in multitiered support systems is shifting to providing expertise about specialized instructional strategies that might benefit any student who is having difficulty learning.

Questions about the role of special educators in inclusive contexts are hardly new, nor are seemingly endless discussions about where students with disabilities should be educated. What is new about special education today is that education as a whole is entering an era of personalized education. In this chapter, we provide a historical overview that situates what is meant by and required of special education in the context of a recent U.S. Supreme Court decision on the education of children with disabilities that raises the bar for the education of learners with disabilities. We close the chapter by discussing changing expectations for educating all students in the 21st century. In Chapter 2 we discuss issues pertaining to changing ways of understanding disability and strengths-based approaches to educating learners with disabilities that also help us to answer the question, What is special education today?

IDEA and the Least Restrictive Environment

To understand what is meant by *special education* and to address the "who" and "where" questions, let's begin at the beginning, with the passage of Public Law 94-142, then titled the Education for All Handicapped Children Act (EHA), in 1975. Within this historical context, the question of "who we teach" is straightforward. Although the disability category areas have expanded, EHA and IDEA define students who are eligible for special education the same way, based on meeting the dual criterion of (a) being identified as a child "with" one of the disabilities categorized in the law (b) who, by virtue of that disability, requires special education to succeed in school. In Chapter 2 we discuss in more depth the standards set for succeeding and the assumptions associated with a child "having" a "disability," but for now, let's leave it here: children who have been identified (through a multidisciplinary, nondiscriminatory evaluation process) as having an eligible disability and who require special education to learn constitute the population of who, historically, special educators teach.

This leads us to a logical next question: if eligible children require special education, what exactly is special education? EHA and, subsequently, IDEA, define *special education* as "specially designed instruction" (regulations to IDEA, 34 C.F.R. §300.39 (a)(1)). *Specially designed instruction* is in turn defined as

> adapting, as appropriate to the needs of an eligible child under this part, the content, methodology, or delivery of instruction—
> (i)　To address the unique needs of the child that result from the child's disability; and
> (ii)　To ensure access of the child to the general curriculum, so that the child can meet the educational standards within the jurisdiction of the public agency that apply to all children (§300.39 (b) (3); https://sites.ed.gov/idea/regs/b/a/300.39)

So, there you have it. Special education means specially designed instruction that adapts *content, methodology,* or *delivery of instruction* to address the *unique* learning needs that result from a child's disability and that ensures access to the general education curriculum.

What "special education" does *not* refer to is a place where students receive instruction (special education room, special education class, etc.), even though it is frequently used as such. Special education, as defined in IDEA, has never been a place; it is the delivery of specialized instruction or content. To examine the

What "special education" does not refer to is a place where students receive instruction (special education room, special education class, etc.), even though it is frequently used as such.

question of where specially designed instruction occurs, we need to consider two elements of EHA/IDEA: (a) the requirements for the provision of supplementary aids and services and (b) the least restrictive environment (LRE) requirements.

Supplementary Aids and Services

Special education (as specially designed instruction) refers to adaptations to delivery of instruction, content, and methodology. EHA and IDEA also require the provision of supplementary aids and services, which the IDEA regulations (§300.42) define as

> aids, services, and other supports that are provided in regular education classes, other education-related settings, and in extracurricular and nonacademic settings, to enable children with disabilities to be educated with nondisabled children to the maximum extent appropriate in accordance with §§300.114 through 300.116. (https://sites.ed.gov/idea/regs/b/a/300.42)

These aids, services, and other supports refer to a wide array of strategies, adaptations, and modifications that are distinct from the adaptations to instruction, content, and methodology comprising specially designed instruction. That is, supplementary aids and services refer to noninstructional modifications and supports/services that support learning. Table 1.1 provides domains pertaining to, the purposes of, and examples of supplementary aids and services.

TABLE 1.1 Supplementary Aids and Services Domains, Purposes, and Examples

DOMAIN	PURPOSE	EXAMPLES
School buildings and facilities	Ensure that all physical spaces are designed to ensure physical, sensory, and cognitive access to enable children with disabilities to be educated with nondisabled children, be involved with and progress in the general education curriculum, and address their unique learning needs	• Elevators • Wide doors • Curb cuts and ramps • Braille and cognitively accessible signage • Accessible restrooms, cafeterias, and other noninstructional facilities

Classrooms and instructional spaces	Ensure that all instructional spaces are designed to ensure physical, sensory, and cognitive access to enable children with disabilities to be educated with nondisabled children, be involved with and progress in the general education curriculum, and address their unique learning needs	• Seating arrangements • Classroom arrangement • Types of seating • Acoustics • Lighting
Instructional technology and equipment	Provide technology and educationally-relevant equipment to enable children with disabilities to be educated with nondisabled children, be involved with and progress in the general education curriculum, and address their unique learning needs	• Computers, tablets, and other educational devices and software • Assistive technology • Augmentative communication device • Calculator • Word processor
Instructional materials and content presentation	Ensure that all instructional materials and the presentation of educational content are universally designed to enable children with disabilities to be educated with nondisabled children, be involved with and progress in the general education curriculum, and address their unique learning needs	• Digital talking books • Advance organizers • Multimedia presentations
Schedules and task modifications	Provide adaptations and modifications to educational schedules, activities, and assessments to enable children with disabilities to be educated with nondisabled children, be involved with and progress in the general education curriculum, and address their unique learning needs	• Extended time • Scribe • Note taker • Oral presentation • Modified reading level • Rest breaks

continued

TABLE 1.1 *continued*

DOMAIN	PURPOSE	EXAMPLES
People	Provide teacher, paraeducator, and peer supports that enable children with disabilities to be educated with nondisabled children, be involved with and progress in the general education curriculum, and address their unique learning needs	• Teacher roles • Paraeducator roles • Peers and classmates roles • Time for collaboration and planning • Training and professional development

So, *special education* refers to adaptations to instruction, methodology, and content; *supplementary aids and services* refer to adaptations and modifications to the context that are distinct from the adaptations to instruction, content, and methodology. IDEA also requires delivery of related services. IDEA (§300.34 (a)) defines related services by, basically, listing a lot of such services:

> Related services means transportation and such developmental, corrective, and other supportive services as are required to assist a child with a disability to benefit from special education, and includes speech-language pathology and audiology services, interpreting services, psychological services, physical and occupational therapy, recreation, including therapeutic recreation, early identification and assessment of disabilities in children, counseling services, including rehabilitation counseling, orientation and mobility services, and medical services for diagnostic or evaluation purposes. Related services also include school health services and school nurse services, social work services in schools, and parent counseling and training. (https://sites.ed.gov/idea/regs/b/a/300.34)

The key to whether students are eligible for related services is whether, as stated in the definition, such services are "required to assist a child with a disability to benefit from special education." We return to the issue of benefit shortly.

Least Restrictive Environment

One of the most frequently misinterpreted requirements in IDEA, in our opinion, pertains to the LRE mandate. Here is how IDEA (§300.114(a)(2)) defines LRE:

> Each public agency must ensure that—
>
> (i) To the maximum extent appropriate, children with disabilities, including children in public or private institutions or other care facilities, are educated with children who are nondisabled; and
>
> (ii) Special classes, separate schooling, or other removal of children with disabilities from the regular educational environment occurs only if the nature or severity of the disability is such that education in regular classes with the use of supplementary aids and services cannot be achieved satisfactorily. (https://sites.ed.gov/idea/regs/b/b/300.114)

Before we explore what the LRE mandate actually means, we have to understand the legal basis for its inclusion in EHA in 1975. The LRE language in IDEA has its origins in the legal principle of least restrictive alternative, which posits that, if the government is going to restrict the liberty and freedom of a citizen in any way, the government has a constitutional obligation to do so "in a way that is least restrictive of the person's liberty itself, in a way that is less drastic than other ways available to the state." Writing only a few years after the full implementation of EHA, Turnbull (1981, p. 26) described least restrictive alternative as "a method of limiting government intrusion into people's lives and rights even when the government is acting in an area which is properly open to governmental action." Let us return now to the LRE language, remembering that public schools are governmental entities and thus must abide by the least restrictive alternative doctrine. The statement that children with disabilities must be educated with children who are nondisabled to the maximum extent appropriate

> Special education *refers to adaptations to instruction, methodology, and content;* supplementary aids and services *refer to adaptations and modifications to the context that are distinct from the adaptations to instruction, content, and methodology.*

is, in essence, a statement of what constitutes the least restrictive alternative. The second part of the LRE statement provides guidance to schools as to what circumstances might constitute a justification for going beyond the least restrictive alternative. That is, removal from regular education environments occurs "only if the nature or severity of the disability is such that education in regular classes with the use of supplementary aids and services cannot be achieved satisfactorily."

Let us look more closely at the justification for removal from regular education environments. The prevailing understanding of this is that the *nature and severity* of a student's disability determines whether that student should be educated somewhere other than the general education setting. That is, most IEP (individualized education program) teams look first at the nature and severity of a student's disability to determine placement within or outside the general education setting (as well as their beliefs about students with certain types of disabilities and levels of impairment). That is certainly how inclusion or exclusion has been practiced over the life of EHA/IDEA, and this is why even today only 17% of students with intellectual disability and fewer than half of students with emotional and behavioral disabilities are educated in general education settings for 80% or more of their day.

However, that is not what the LRE language says. It states that removal from regular education environments occurs *only if* students cannot be successful in regular education

> Removal from regular education environments occurs "only if the nature or severity of the disability is such that education in regular classes with the use of supplementary aids and services cannot be achieved satisfactorily.

environments with the use of supplementary aids and services. This tells us a couple of things. First, that special education (e.g., specially designed instruction) was not mentioned in the LRE statement indicates that adapting the delivery of instruction, content, and methodology is not specific to the context in which students are educated. Second, it tells us that the context in which the federal law prioritizes instruction is the regular education environment, with students in that context supported with supplementary aids and series (such as those listed in Table 1.1) so that students can benefit from specially designed instruction in regular education environments. And, just to wrap up the discussion about terms in the LRE requirements, officials in the U.S. Department of Education's Office of Special Education Programs, which implements regulations pertaining to IDEA, issued guidance defining "regular education environments" as encompassing "regular classrooms and other settings in schools such as lunchrooms and playgrounds in which children without disabilities participate" (71 *Fed. Reg.* 46585, 2006).

Thus, where special educators should be teaching, in our estimation, should be in the least restrictive environment, which IDEA refers to as regular educational environments. Special educators are responsible for providing specially designed instruction and implementing supplementary aids and services in regular educational settings as a default context. Only if a student is not successful in such a context should the decision to remove that student be considered. And, as will be fleshed out in this book and in subsequent books in the Norton Inclusive Education for Students With Disabilities series, with advances in schoolwide and multitiered systems of supports, in technology and universal design for learning, in the increasing presence of personalized learning for all students, and in myriad other factors, there is the promise and potential that every child can receive an *appropriately* ambitious education that considers each child's potential for growth.

Beyond De Minimis

At the end of the preceding section, we intentionally used the terms *appropriately ambitious education* and *potential for growth*. We drew these terms from a 2017 U.S. Supreme Court ruling that established what constituted *appropriate* and *beneficial* educational programs as required by IDEA and that provides part of the answer to what special education is in an inclusive and strengths-based era. First, it is important to understand how the requirements for an appropriate education (as in a free, appropriate public education, which is what IDEA requires) have been interpreted for much of the lifetime of IDEA.

In 1982, the U.S. Supreme Court issued a decision in *Board of Education of the Hendrick Hudson Central School District v. Rowley* (458 U.S. 176) that established a standard for what constituted an appropriate education for students with disabilities for the next 25 years. The Court held that the EHA did not require a state to "maximize the potential of each handicapped child commensurate with the opportunity provided nonhandicapped children." Rather, the state need only provide "specialized instruction and related services which are individually designed to provide educational benefit to the handicapped child." That is, a school district was obligated not to develop an IEP that would encourage a student with a disability to achieve his or her academic best, or to provide the best possible program, but merely to provide one that might reasonably be thought to benefit the student in some way (Weatherly & Conrad, 2016).

The problems with this standard are myriad. For one, what constitutes a "program designed to provide educational benefit" becomes, by and large, a paperwork standard: considerable effort was placed on documenting that schools were in compliance with procedures stipulated in EHA/IDEA. Also, what constitutes educational benefit is in the eye of the beholder, and if educators and others hold low expectations for students, then programs based even on "student potential" can have little or no meaningful benefit.

Enter Endrew F., a student diagnosed with autism at two years of age. As described in Turnbull et al. (2019), Endrew entered preschool in a school district in Colorado and transitioned from preschool to elementary school. By Endrew's fourth grade year, however, his parents had become dissatisfied with his progress or, in their opinion, his lack thereof. He engaged in behaviors that disrupted his learning, including screaming in class, climbing over furniture, and on occasion running away from school. His parents were frustrated because, in their opinion, his IEP had the same goals and objectives year after year, and he was not making meaningful progress toward even those repetitive goals. When, in April 2010, the district presented Endrew's parents with a proposed IEP for his fifth grade year that in their opinion was just more of the same, they withdrew Endrew from public school and enrolled him in a private school for children with autism.

Endrew did progress at the new school, which implemented a behavioral intervention plan to address his behavioral issues and instituted more challenging academic goals for him. Endrew's parents took the information about his progress, and how it had been achieved, back to the public school district with the intention to move Endrew back to the public school and receive the beneficial educational program implemented in the private school. Instead, they were presented with an IEP that, in their viewpoint, simply repeated what had been offered in April 2010; they rejected it and kept Endrew at the private school. In

February 2012, Endrew's parents filed a complaint with the state Department of Education seeking reimbursement for the tuition they paid to the private school. The standard they had to meet, legally, to be reimbursed was that the school district had not provided a free, appropriate public education prior to his enrollment in the private school. As per *Rowley*, they contended that the final IEP they had received was not reasonably calculated to enable Endrew to receive educational benefits. Beginning with a mediator and then in decisions by the federal district court and the Tenth Circuit Court, the determination was that, while it was clear that Endrew did not evidence much educational growth and progress, the annual IEPs provided by the public school did evidence a pattern of minimal progress.

In January 2017, lawyers for the family and the school district argued their sides before the U.S. Supreme Court. In their report, issued in March 2017, the Court summarized the Tenth Circuit Court's decision as noting that

> it had long interpreted this language [referring to *Rowley*] to mean that a child's IEP is adequate as long as it is calculated to confer an "educational benefit [that is] merely . . . more than *de minimis*." Applying this standard, the Tenth Circuit held that Endrew's IEP had been "reasonably calculated to enable [him] to make *some* progress." (137 S. Ct. 988 [2017])

De minimis is a term used in law and accounting to mean lacking in significance, importance, or value. Thus, the Supreme Court was summarizing the decisions that preceded the *Endrew F.* case, both previous court rulings in this specific case and, more generally, lower courts' rulings in the wake of *Rowley*, as requiring only benefit that exceeded minimal progress.

In considering the arguments before them in *Endrew F.*, the Supreme Court justices concluded that,

> when all is said and done, a student offered an educational program providing "merely more than *de minimis*" progress from year to year can hardly be said to have been offered an education at all. For children with disabilities, receiving instruction that aims so low would be tantamount to "sitting idly . . . awaiting the time when they were old enough to 'drop out.'" . . . It requires an educational program reasonably calculated to enable a child to make progress appropriate in light of the child's

circumstances." (https://www.supremecourt.gov/opinions/16pdf/15
-827_0pm1.pdf, p. 14).

The *Endrew F.* ruling established new standards for what is an appropriate education, stating the following:

- A child's educational program must be *appropriately ambitious* [emphasis
  added] in light of the child's circumstances. (p. 3)
- Goals may differ, but every child should have the chance to meet *challenging objectives* [emphasis added]. (p. 3)
- An IEP is not a form document. It is constructed only after consideration of the child's present levels of achievement, disability, and *potential
  for growth* [emphasis added]. (p. 12)
- The adequacy of a given IEP turns on the unique circumstances of the
  child for whom it was created. (p. 13)

Fundamentally, in *Endrew F.*, the U.S. Supreme Court changed how an appropriate or beneficial education is understood. A child's educational program must be
appropriately ambitious, and every child should have the opportunity to meet
challenging objectives. An educational program must be appropriately ambitious
in light of that child's circumstances; rather than rely solely on present levels of
achievement and the child's disability, the program must take into consideration
the child's potential for growth and the child's unique circumstances.

Not only do the *Endrew F.* standards raise the bar well above *de minimis*; it
also, in our opinion, aligns the education of learners with disabilities closely with
personalized learning in general, as we noted at the start of this chapter. That
is, a child's educational pro-
gram should be appropri-
ately ambitious and provide
challenging objectives, be
based on the child's unique
circumstances—including
the child's unique interests,
abilities, strengths, and instructional needs—and take into account a child's
potential for growth. In an age of personalized learning and strengths-based
approaches, that formula could apply to almost every child in school.

> *Rather than rely solely on present levels of
> achievement and the child's disability,
> the program must take into consideration the
> child's potential for growth and the child's
> unique circumstances.*

Conclusion

In this chapter, we began by posing the question, What is special education today? We have suggested pieces of the answer to that question. First, we need to understand that special education is specially designed instruction and not a place where students are sent and that, in an era of dramatic educational reformation, the tools, knowledge, and strategies that special educators hold should be part of the educational system's efforts to personalize learning and to promote student agency. Like all aspects of education, the context of special education has changed and, more important, continues to rapidly evolve. Education is responding to changing, global demands for students to master skills such as communication, creativity, critical thinking, problem solving, and collaboration. It is doing so by providing increasingly personalized learning opportunities; promoting student agency and enhancing motivation by focusing on students' strengths and interests; leveraging technology; and moving away from the notion that all children need to acquire a single set of skills to be successful. These trends are as important to special education as to general education and we will highlight issues pertaining to them in greater detail throughout the book.

Second, we have suggested that IDEA has an unambiguous preference for educating children with disabilities in regular education environments, compelled by the LRE doctrine. Although it has too often not been interpreted as such, the LRE requirement in IDEA makes it clear that removal from regular education environments should occur only when the student cannot be successful when provided supplementary aids and services and specially designed instruction. Further, there has been steady, if at times incremental, progress in achieving the preference that learners with disabilities be educated in regular education environments with their nondisabled peers. The field has already recognized that we need to focus on schoolwide approaches to educating learners with disabilities, leveraging technology and universal design to ensure access, and emphasizing student agency and self-determination. These goals are important in the education of all children, require educators who have skills to individualize learning, and, logically, are best situated in regular education environments.

We need to ask why some children continue to be excluded from high-quality instruction in regular education environments. One part of the answer we have proposed here is that the LRE requirement has been misinterpreted to mean that the nature and severity of a child's disability should be considered when making placement decisions. But this is counter to the LRE requirement for removal only if students cannot be educated successfully in typical educational settings with a wide array of supports and services; to the higher expectations for involvement with and progress in the general education curriculum in IDEA; and, seemingly, to the Supreme Court's expectations in *Endrew F.* that every child's educational program must be appropriately ambitious, that every child should have the opportunity to meet challenging objectives, and that IEPs should take into consideration the child's potential for growth and unique circumstances.

Reflective Questions for Group Study

1. What factors have influenced the interpretation of the least restrictive environment requirements in IDEA?
2. What global educational trends are influencing the education of students with disabilities?
3. How does the Supreme Court ruling in Endrew change how we understand a "free appropriate public education"?

2

Can We Broaden Our Reach?

Strengths-Based Approaches to Disability

This chapter addresses the question of why children with disabilities continue to be held to low expectations and to be educated in segregated settings. To understand how to answer the central question of Chapter 1, What is special education?, in an inclusive and strengths-based era, we went back to Public Law 94-142, the 1975 Education for All Handicapped Children Act (EHA), which is the precursor to the 2004 Individuals With Disabilities Education Act (IDEA). Likewise, in understanding why children with disabilities continue to be segregated and held to low expectations, we again begin with the EHA.

The question of who we teach as it pertains to special education dates back to the days following the passage of the EHA. Lance (1976) published an article asking who the "all" in the Education for All Handicapped Children Act were. In that article, published only one year after EHA was signed into legislation and two years before it was required to be fully implemented, Lance identified the reason for the establishment of special education as "the recognition of the need to provide different treatments to individuals with obviously differing capacities for benefiting from the traditional educational practices" (p. 68). In his discussion, Lance cited a 1974 resolution from the Council for Exceptional Children as stating that children who did not have such access were "children for whom educators have responsibilities to assist in prevention of further injury and to provide programs to remediate the damage that has occurred" (p. 72).

Wehmeyer (2019) noted that this description was typical of how the purpose of the EHA and special education was discussed at the time the law was passed and that the bulk of these discussions used terms like those used by Lance and CEC: *treatment, prevention, damage,* and *reduction of injury.* All of these are medical terms. The purpose of EHA was to *treat* children with disabilities, who were understood solely in medical terms at the time: to *prevent* future *impairment* and *disability* and to *reduce injury, damage,* and *harm* from the disability. These purposes were consistent with how disability was understood at that time, and in this chapter we focus on the issue of how disability was and is understood and how changes to such understandings benefit inclusive and personalized education.

Understanding Disability

Let us first establish that how we understand disability has a direct and causal impact on how we design interventions to support people whom we determine have that disability. This is so much the case that we often name or describe the eras of disability history in the dual terms associated with how disability was understood and the associated treatment paradigm. Thus, Thompson et al. (2017) identified the two overarching historic paradigms in disability services as the medical/institutional paradigm and the normalization/community services paradigm. Both, however, were predicated on a biomedical model of disability.

> *Rather than rely solely on present levels of achievement and the child's disability, the program must take into consideration the child's potential for growth and the child's unique circumstances.*

Biomedical Models of Disability

The task of defining disability for the first century of the history of the field of disability services was left to the professionals who had established the field and created the first systems of services. These were medical professionals who adhered to biomedical models of disability. Simply speaking, such models view disability within the context of long-term or chronic health conditions and as an internal pathology, resulting from disease or impairment (Wehmeyer, 2013). The interventions or treatments derived from such an understanding are, not surprisingly, medically oriented. The early history of disability is one of the development and expansion of hospitals and institutions implementing treatments designed by medical professionals using medical models and medical practices (Smith & Wehmeyer, 2012). While originally intended to be habilitative, these services became increasingly segregated, involving larger and larger congregate settings with the purpose of, at their best, protection and care and, at their worst, isolation and restriction.

By the mid-20th century, the professionalization of the disability field had proliferated to include psychologists, therapists of all kinds, educators, support staff, and others, all of whom operated within biomedical understandings of disability. Eventually, the abuses and flaws of these historic institutional paradigms became so obvious that family members (mostly parents, along with some professionals) began to demand something different (Abeson & Davis, 2000). Buoyed by the post-World War II zeitgeist that anything was possible, these advocates created a community-based system of services that, by the end of the century, had radically changed where people with disability lived. They did this through the courts, through legislation, and through the creation of innovative supports. They also created the opportunity for children with disabilities to attend school. It was this so-called parent movement that, in essence, established what we now call IDEA.

And yet, despite all the progress made during this post-World War II era, how disability was understood fundamentally did not change. It continued to be understood within the biomedical model in which disability was conceptualized in terms of pathology, defects, and deficits. The newly established special education system thus inherited an understanding of disability as pathology and deficit and created an educational version of the medical model of services: separate and segregated classrooms and buildings where practitioners emphasized (back to Lance, 1976) treatment, prevention, and reduction of damage and injury.

Social Models of Disability

There was movement afoot, however, to change how disability was understood, and it was initiated within the medical system itself. Medical professionals concluded that there were limitations to conceptualizing long-term or chronic health care issues (including disability) within a disease and deficit model. In 1980, the World Health Organization (WHO) introduced the International Classification of Impairments, Disabilities, and Handicaps (ICIDH). Prior to this, the WHO included disability (across various categories) as a disease or a disorder, but the

ICIDH broke away from this. The ICIDH was intended not as a classification of diseases or disorders but as a means to classify the consequences of disease, injuries, and other disorders and of their implications for the lives of the people affected. For the first time, at least at a large-scale, systematic level, disability was recognized not simply as a function of health problems but instead as a function of interactions among and relationships between health-related issues, the context in which the person wants to function, and the characteristics of the person.

In 2001, the WHO took these ideas a step further, introducing the International Classification of Functioning, Disability, and Health (ICF). The ICF extended this understanding of disability as a function of the interrelationships between and among health, environmental, and personal factors and conceptualized disability as a part of, and not apart from, typical human functioning. Models of disability such as the ICF

Disability resides only in the gap between what people can do and what they want to do.

are identified as social-ecological or person-environment fit models because they shift the locus of disability from within the person (as was the case in the biomedical model) to the gap between the person's abilities and capacities and the demands of the environment. That is, disability resides only in the gap between what people can do and what they want to do (Buntinx, 2013).

A second, and perhaps more important, movement was emerging at the same time: the disability rights movement. The parent era established critical civil rights legislation, including the right to a free, appropriate public education. At the same time, people with disabilities were coming together to create a disability rights and self-advocacy movement (Driedger, 1989). One emphasis within this rights-based self-advocacy movement was the "advancement of a positive disability identity and culture" (Caldwell, 2011). Longmore (2003) called the establishment of disability identity and culture the second phase of the disability rights movement, and Longmore and Umansky (2001) argued that,

> while public policy has sought to fashion disability as a generic category
> and attempted to impose that classification of people with an assortment
> of conditions, disability has never been a monolithic grouping. There
> has always been a variety of disability experiences. [These] experiences
> of cultural devaluation and socially imposed restriction, of personal and

collective struggles for self-definition and self-determination—recur across the various disability groups and throughout their personal histories. (p. 4)

Leaders in the disability rights and self-advocacy movement emphasize that, by embracing disability identity, they recapture their personhood and lay claim to social justice, full citizenship, and participation. What emerged from this movement was what is referred to as a social model of disability, which views disability as arising "from the discrimination and disadvantage individuals experience in relation to others because of their particular differences and characteristics" (Bach, 2017, p. 40). Within a social model,

> the unit of analysis shifts from the individual to the legal, social, economic, and political structures that calculate value and status on the basis of difference. Informed by principles of human rights, and an equality of outcomes that takes account of differences, the social model does not reject bio-medical knowledge of impairments and research on individual rehabilitation. Rather, it celebrates impairment as part of the human condition, and looks at achieving equity for people with impairments in terms of the social, cultural, and political contexts. (Bach, 2017, p. 40)

Social-ecological or person-environment fit models of disability are situated within the broader context of social models. There is some tension among advocates who emphasize the identity aspects of disability and ascribe to a pure social model and the social-ecological models that evolved from the medical system. For one, the latter still include medical and health formulations in the understanding of disability. However, while these differences are important, and we support the movement to embrace disability as identity, a social-ecological model lends itself better to education and the development of interventions and supports. And, among the many points of agreement between social and social-ecological models, a critically important one is that we cannot understand disability without taking into account people's strengths and abilities and the contexts in which people live, learn, work, and play.

We cannot understand disability without taking into account people's strengths and abilities and the contexts in which people live, learn, work, and play.

"Having" a Disability: An Outdated Phrase

In Chapter 1 we briefly discussed how IDEA identifies students who are eligible for special education services. Basically, eligibility requires that students meet the definition of one of the disability categorical areas and need specially designed instruction to be successful. We want to use this requirement to briefly consider the notion of a person "having" a disability. When disability was understood within a biomedical model, it was logical to refer to someone as having a disability, since it was understood that the locus of the disability was within the person. But when we view disability as a function of the environment and context, as does the social model, or as the interaction between personal capacity and the demands of the environment, as does the person-environment fit model, the locus of the disability lies outside of the person—the person does not *have* a disability. In the social model, disability is something imposed on people by environments, contexts, and systems. In social-ecological or person-environment fit models, disability resides in the gap between what someone can do and what someone wants to do.

In the next section, we discuss implications for these changing understandings of disability for inclusive education. But before we enumerate some of these implications, we want to note that, as long as our society continues to see people as "having" disability, then we in essence perpetuate biomedical notions of disease, pathology, and deficits. In a similar manner, if we continue to adhere to IDEA's process of eligibility for specially designed instruction because of "diagnosis" of a disability, we in turn perpetuate a system of segregation and discrimination. The solution is to adopt educational practices that focus on all children, are strengths based, emphasize universal design, focus on schoolwide approaches that provide high-quality instruction for all students, emphasize student agency and self-determined learning, abandon the notion of average as useful, and ensure personalized education for all children. These are the focal points for the next section.

Implications for Inclusive Education

To consider how changing understandings of disability impact inclusive education, we focus on social-ecological or, as we prefer, person-environment fit models of disability. These models begin with a person's strengths and capacities and then consider what is needed to function successfully in the environments and contexts in which that person wants to function. As noted, while we understand

and fully endorse disability as identity and pure social models of disability, the fact is that education is an intervention-oriented enterprise. Our role as educators is to improve student knowledge and skills so that students can be successful. As such, the person-environment fit model provides multiple ways we can proceed to design such interventions: we can provide learning opportunities that enable students to enhance their skills and knowledge needed to function successfully in the preferred context; we can modify the context in ways that enable the person to perform successfully; and we can provide supports that enable the person to be successful. The good news is that a number of approaches, practices, and mindsets in special and inclusive education already conform with or are driven by person-environment fit models of disability, beginning with a strengths-based approach.

Strengths-Based Approaches

Person-environment fit models require that we begin by considering a student's strengths, abilities, and competencies. Historically, deficits and remedial approaches began with just the opposite: a determination of the student's deficits. Strengths-based approaches take, as a starting point, the assumptions of social models of disability and then translate them into approaches to support, educate, or enable students with disabilities to function successfully in typical contexts. There is considerable power in beginning with a student's strengths, among them that it can enhance a positive relationship between the student and the teacher.

The social models and strengths-based approaches lead to a support focus in inclusive education. Deficit-based models led to the development of "programs" that were predicated on the type or severity of the person's disability. Within person-environment fit models and strengths-based approaches, we are interested in identifying what supports a student needs, where supports are defined as anything that can enhance functioning and self-determination to enable a person to be successful. We return to this later in this book when we discuss personalizable education and student agency.

Schoolwide Approaches

There is an increasing recognition that the focus for inclusive education should be at the school level rather than simply at the classroom level. Schools are communities that involve an array of students with differing experiences, abilities, and interests. The prevalent schoolwide approach in place now involves multitiered systems of supports (MTSS). An MTSS framework emerged from the combination of "tiered" interventions to address the needs of students who were struggling, academically, referred to as "response to intervention" (Fuchs et al., 2010), and to address students who were struggling behaviorally, through school-wide positive behavior support (Horner & Sugai, 2015).

In an MTSS model, all students receive high-quality, evidence-based, and universally designed instruction, referred to as tier 1 instruction, taking into consideration their linguistic and cultural backgrounds, abilities, and other areas of learning support needs. Historically, if students were struggling to learn, they would be "referred" to special education, which too often meant going somewhere other than the general education classroom for either part or all of the day. In MTSS models, consistent with person-environment fit models, what changes when students are struggling is the type, intensity, or duration of instruction.

Thus, some students may receive what is referred to as tier 2 instruction, which changes the instruction in some way but not where the student receives that instruction.

In MTSS models, what changes when students are struggling is the type, intensity, or duration of instruction.

Finally, a few students may need more individualized, intensive supports to succeed, referred to as tier 3 supports. But it is important to understand that, throughout this process, as students move to more intensive levels (tiers) of support, they do not need to be removed from general education classes—again, what changes is the type, intensity, or duration of instruction.

The U.S. Department of Education's Office of Special Education Programs funded a national K–8 technical assistance center at the University of Kansas called the Schoolwide Integrated Framework for Transformation (SWIFT) Center, that emphasizes state- and district-level commitment to the education of all learners within a multitiered approach. The SWIFT model of MTSS emphasizes research-based, data-driven decisions to determine the type and intensity of instructional supports needed by students with disabilities. The model presumes that all students are involved in high-quality instruction and that data are available from all students to inform instructional decisions (McCart et al., 2014). A future book in the Norton Inclusive Education for Students With Disabilities series will focus on the SWIFT model and provide more detail about schoolwide approaches to promote inclusive education.

Universal Design for Learning

A second illustration of how person-environment fit models of disability can impact practice in education involves the application of universal design for learning (UDL). Orkwis and McLane (1998, p. 9) defined UDL as "the design of instructional materials and activities that allows the learning goals to be achievable by individuals with wide differences in their abilities to see, hear, speak, move, read, write, understand English, attend, organize, engage, and remember." First, then, UDL is about the design of instructional materials and is a form of supplementary aids and services. Such materials are designed in ways that allow all students to benefit from the material. Think of it this way: If a student had difficulty reading and is in a sixth-grade language arts class where the rest of the class is reading one of the myriad young adult novels taught in that grade, simply providing a copy of the print book will be of little use to that student. We can, however, adjust how the content of that book is represented—say, provide it in digital format so the student can "read" the book using a digital talking book—that ensures the student can participate with other students in the class. Further, universally designed materials benefit a lot of students, not just students with disabilities.

Self-Determination

The focus on transition in the education of learners receiving special education services emerged in the 1980s as the first wave of students served under the EHA began to exit school to more and less optimal outcomes: more in that outcomes like employment and community inclusion improved as a function of the access to education that the EHA provided; less in that those improvements were incremental and fell short of what had been hoped for (Wehmeyer & Webb, 2012). One issue identified as potentially contributing to these less positive than expected outcomes was that students were not actively engaged in the transition process. As a result, the U.S. Department of Education's Office of Special Education Programs began a number of initiatives to remedy this, including a focus in the reauthorization of the EHA, renamed IDEA, on transition and student involvement in transition planning (Wehmeyer & Ward, 1995).

From these initiatives emerged a focus on promoting the self-determination of young people receiving special education services. Over the past three decades, evidence has accumulated on the importance of enhanced self-determination to more positive school-related performance and transition-to-adulthood outcomes. Further, evidence-based interventions and assessments have been developed and implemented to enable teachers to promote student self-determination (Shogren & Wehmeyer, 2020). A focus on self-determination is important both for personalized education, as discussed in Chapter 1, and in the context of person-environment fit models and strengths-based approaches. In personalized education, students will have to become owners of their own learning; they will need to be able to identify what they do well and what they are interested in and use problem-solving and goal-setting skills along with this knowledge to chart their own path toward their future. In the fields of vocational and career guidance and counseling and, more recently, in the field of transition services within special education, professionals are increasingly adopting a life design approach (described in Chapter 5), which empha-

Strengths-based approaches place the student at the center of all learning.

sizes students designing and constructing their own careers and lives (Wehmeyer et al., 2019). Acting in a self-determined manner is central to these processes.

Further, strengths-based approaches place the student at the center of all learning. As we head into an era of personalized learning, student self-determined learning becomes critical to positive outcomes. We return to this in greater detail in Chapter 5.

Strengths-Based Approaches and Inclusive Education

Throughout the books in this series we will explore and expand on ideas introduced in this chapter to understand such topics as schoolwide approaches, universal design, supports, and self-determination, so as to "broaden our reach" with regard to inclusive education. In Chapters 3 and 4 we do a deeper dive into what we know about effective practices in inclusive education and evidence in support of inclusive education. In the final chapter we return to some of the issues to look at where we go from here in inclusive education. For now, it is worth asking what a strengths-based approach predicated on social models of disability gets us as educators interested in inclusive education.

First, in Chapter 1 we discussed the implications for special education aris-ing from the *Endrew F.* Supreme Court decision. As a field, we cannot achieve the standards of an appropriately ambitious education that is based on a student's potential for growth unless we jettison deficit-focused educational practices and embrace strengths-based approaches. How we understand disability does matter when it comes to what we do "about" disability. As we asked at the beginning of this chapter, why is it that, even though the EHA and IDEA emphasize educat-ing students with disabilities with their nondisabled peers, we are still struggling, almost 50 years later, to achieve that vision? In part, it is because how we have conceptualized disability most of those 50 years viewed students as incapable and incompetent.

In the 1997 reauthorization of IDEA, language was introduced that required schools to ensure that all students receiving special education services were involved with and progressing in the general education curriculum. These so-called "access to the general education curriculum" mandates were introduced to align the education of learners receiving special education services with (at that time) prevailing standards-based reform efforts. Independent of how one feels about that era and its concomitant emphasis on standards, accountability, and testing, one useful thing as we move forward is that these actions were under-taken to raise expectations for students receiving special education services, expectations that historically had been low (Lee et al., 2008; Wehmeyer, 2006). Strengths-based approaches allow us to move forward and to presume that stu-dents with disabilities can be successful and that we can have high expectations for them.

These social-ecological or person-environment fit models emphasize that disability is part of, and not apart from, typical human functioning. The WHO ICF and the social and identity models emphasize participation as a critical ele-ment of understanding disability. That is, disability is best understood in these models by looking at the participation of people with disabilities in all aspects of life. It is, in fact, the impact of health, environmental, and personal factors on a person's activities and full participation that defines disability. If someone is fully participating, even with accommodations and supports, then under the ICF model, while the impairment may still be there, disability is essentially irrelevant.

Thus, trends in personalized education and changing understandings of dis-ability make inclusive education even more important, and in adopting strengths-based approaches and their related instructional models and strategies, we can break the logjam with regard to fulfilling IDEA's expectations for the education of learners with disabilities.

Reflective Questions for Group Study

1. Compare and contrast social models and social-ecological models of disability and discuss the relative benefits of each.
2. How does a strengths-based approach to educating learners with disabilities change how education is structured?
3. Consider current special educational practices and discuss which such practices fit within social-ecological models of disability.

3

How Can We Teach Better?

Effective Practices in Inclusive Schools and Classrooms

In this chapter, we turn our attention to effective inclusive instructional practices. As described in preceding chapters, both strengths-based approaches (Chapter 2) and instruction in the regular education environment (Chapter 1) are essential to promoting positive student outcomes. To respond to the question, How can we teach better?, it is important to first establish that students with disabilities deserve, and require, effective instruction. Too often, expectations have been woefully low for both students with disabilities and their teachers. Low expectations, in the form of watered down and disjointed curricula, unambitious learning goals, and few opportunities to learn, have resulted in millions of students leaving school without the skills to be successful in adult life. In fact, students with disabilities have the lowest rates of postsecondary education and full-time employment (Smith et al., 2017), suggesting the need to provide improved education services to better prepare students for life after high school. To counter these low expectations and improve instruction for students with disabilities in inclusive settings, educators must identify and use effective teaching practices that both raise expectations and promote positive outcomes. In this chapter, we describe five effective practices: family-school partnerships, instructional strategies, teaching arrangements, teaching strategies, and technology in inclusive classrooms.

Family-School Partnerships

Family-school partnerships are defined as parents and professionals working together to design and implement education programs (Blue-Banning et al., 2004). This often includes working together to design and implement individualized education programs (IEPs) and monitoring student progress toward shared goals for students. Families are essential team members in these processes.

Partnerships and Why They Matter

Forming trusting, reciprocal partnerships is a critical ingredient in student success; these relationships enhance joint problem solving, communication, planning, and implementation of supports and services, all of which contribute to shared purpose and efforts to benefit students (Hoy, 2012; Newman, 2005). As lifelong allies, family members can also help educators set ambitious expectations for students. However, because parents are usually not as familiar with special education procedures and jargon as are school professionals, an equitable partnership can be challenging to establish (Hess et al., 2006). In fact, many parents report feeling that they are unheard, have little power, and lack information to be effective partners (Love et al., 2017). Therefore, an investment in the family-school partnership is needed to help teams, which include family members and educators, set high expectations and promote positive student outcomes. Table 3.1 provides an overview of essential characteristics of effective family-school partnerships, along with suggested activities for each domain (Blue-Banning et al., 2004; Haines et al., 2015).

TABLE 3.1 Key Characteristics of Effective Family-School Partnerships

DOMAIN	INDICATORS	EXAMPLE ACTIVITIES
Communication	• Sharing resources, such as curricular materials and information about students at home • Clear and honest communication; avoid jargon • Listen carefully • Solicit information from families • Be honest and tactful • Be cognizant of your nonverbal communication	Start the school year by asking families their preferred mode and frequency of communication. Offer several options, including phone calls, written notes, emails, recorded videos, and video conferences.

Commitment	<ul><li>Encourage the student and family</li><li>Be accessible</li><li>Be consistent</li><li>Be sensitive</li></ul>	Share your hopes and expectations for the student. Be specific and optimistic. Share your plan for achieving those goals and how you will adjust your strategies as needed to achieve the goals you set for yourself as an educator.
Equality	<ul><li>Empower partners with information and status</li><li>Validate others</li><li>Advocate for the student or family</li><li>Explore all options</li></ul>	Avoid sending home drafts of IEPs; instead, provide families with data about student progress. This enables all stakeholders to have equality in terms of information and status in development of IEPs.
Skills	<ul><li>Be willing to learn and try</li><li>Have high expectations of the student</li><li>Take action when needed</li></ul>	Individualize supports and services to students; have a plan for adapting those supports and services as needed over time. Solicit input and feedback from families and other professionals, as well as professional development, to continue to work to meet student needs and solve problems as they inevitably arise.
Trust	<ul><li>Be reliable</li><li>Keep the student safe</li><li>Be discrete</li></ul>	Call families periodically to share good news about the student—too often, families only hear about problems. Establish yourself as a person who is a trusting cheerleader for the student and family.

continued

TABLE 3.1 *continued*

DOMAIN	INDICATORS	EXAMPLE ACTIVITIES
Respect	• Value the student • Use a strengths-based mindset • Be courteous • Hold high expectations of students and families • Avoid discrimination	Model language and behaviors that promote the dignity, worth, and value of students and families.

Forming Partnerships

To reap the rewards of trusting family-school partnerships, these relationships must first be formed. Doing so takes both time and effort, but as mentioned previously, the positive student outcomes make the effort worthwhile. Burke et al. (2016) identified three key steps for forming effective partnerships with families.

The first is listening to the family. All families are likely to have previous experiences interacting with professionals (e.g., medical doctors, previous teachers, administrators) that will affect their relationship with you. Be open to listening to those stories, and hear what the family needs and hopes for in their new partnership with you; listen for stories of things that did or did not work in those previous relationships. Your listening also demonstrates your interest in the family and student, as well as your commitment to the student and this partnership.

Working with families to promote meaningful student involvement in and ownership over educational planning and educational decisions is critical to personalized education and inclusion.

Second, establish clear expectations in terms of the partnership. Make sure to clarify your hopes and expectations for the student and your partnership with the family. Be clear that you will seek information and support from others, as needed, to meet these expectations. And clarify how you will communicate, and when.

Third, focus on empowering the family and sustaining an equitable partnership. This means sharing information and ideas and asking families questions. It also means seeking and acting on information, ideas, and insights from families. Maintaining frequent, trusting, and mutually respectful communication will establish an important foundation for continued family-school partnerships. And, of course, students are part of families, and working with families to promote meaningful student involvement in and ownership over educational planning and educational decisions is critical to personalized education and inclusion.

Instructional Strategies

As articulated in Chapter 1, special education is the provision of specially designed instruction. This instruction should be effective, ambitious, strengths based, and designed to maximize student learning outcomes. How does one know what instruction meets these criteria? One of the clearest indicators is that an instructional strategy is supported by research. In fact, the 2004 Individuals With Disabilities Education Act (IDEA) mandated that IEP teams make instructional decisions based on research. IDEA specifies that this research must reflect regular education environments where children receive special education services and demonstrate effectiveness in improving results for students with disabilities. However, educators must also make sure that instructional strategies are personalized to meet the unique learning needs of particular students. Thus, a one-size-fits-all approach is simply inappropriate. The most complete list of practices educators should use are referred to as high-leverage practices (HLPs). They are considered high leverage because they can be used across different content areas and grade levels and constitute the "common core of professional knowledge and skill" to support effective teaching and improved student outcomes (Ball & Forzani, 2011, p. 19).

The HLPs were developed based on extensive review of the research by experts in special education (McLeskey et al., 2017) and are likely to be effective in promoting positive student outcomes across content areas and grade levels. The HLPs are organized around four practice aspects: collaboration, assessment, social/emotional/behavioral practices, and instruction. HLPs in these four practice aspects are integrated and reciprocal, in that all aspects work together to support teaching and learning. For example, teachers use assessment to design and evaluate instruction in all aspects (e.g., academic content, behavior, so cial skills), and teachers use their knowledge of HLPs when they collaborate with others. A total of 22 HLPs were identified within the four practice aspects; these HLPs can be accessed online at https://highleveragepractices.org/about-hlps/.

TABLE 3.2 Twenty-Two High Leverage Practices (HLPs)

HLP #	HLP TITLE
Collaboration Aspect	
1	Collaborate with professionals to increase student success
2	Organize and facilitate effective meetings with professionals and families.
3	Collaborate with families to support student learning and secure needed services.
Assessment Aspect	
4	Use multiple sources of information to develop a comprehensive understanding of a student's strengths and needs.
5	Interpret and communicate assessment information with stakeholders to collaboratively design and implement educational programs.
6	Use student assessment data, analyze instructional practices, and make necessary adjustments that improve student outcomes
Social/Emotional Behavioral Practices Aspect	
7	Establish a consistent, organized, and respectful learning environment
8	Provide positive and constructive feedback to guide students' learning and behavior
9	Teach social behaviors
10	Conduct functional behavioral assessments to develop individual student behavior support plans
Instruction Aspect	
11	Identify and prioritize long- and short-term learning goals
12	Systematically design instruction toward a specific learning goal
13	Adapt curriculum tasks and materials for specific learning goals
14	Teach cognitive and metacognitive strategies to support learning and independence
15	Provide scaffolded supports
16	Use explicit instruction
17	Use flexible grouping
18	Use strategies to promote active student engagement.
19	Use assistive and instructional technologies
20	Provide intensive instruction
21	Teach students to maintain and generalize new learning across time and settings
22	Provide positive and constructive feedback to guide students' learning and behavior

Teaching Arrangements in Inclusive Education

Upon selection and personalization of effective, research-based instructional strategies, educators must then go about the work of implementing them in inclusive settings. This will necessarily rely on knowledge of the general education curriculum and the routines and activities of the general education classroom. As such, collaboration is integral to effective inclusive instruction. Earlier in this chapter, we discussed the importance of family-professional partnership. Here, we turn our attention to interprofessional collaboration as an essential component of teaching students with disabilities. We then discuss the roles and responsibilities of varied professionals in the inclusive classroom.

Interprofessional Collaboration

Interprofessional collaboration refers to two or more professionals working together toward a common goal. Considering the varied team members who interact with students receiving special education services, interprofessional collaboration occurs between people with different background knowledge, experience, and sometimes values. For example, a speech language pathologist and special education teacher may approach a problem from two very different perspectives, even though they share the same goal of supporting the student. Often, professionals are also stretched for time and resources, amounting to another potential obstacle to effective collaboration. However, interprofessional collaboration can be enormously beneficial to students. For one, the multiple perspectives of professionals may present new solutions that one person working with a student may not have considered. Interprofessional collaboration can also improve student outcomes by integrating the strengths and expertise of several professionals who support one another to deliver instruction, giving the student a team of experts to learn from. Finally, interprofessional collaboration allows teachers, who are being tasked with a wider range of responsibilities in today's schools, to rely on support from others to complete their responsibilities.

Interprofessional collaboration relies on shared perspectives and goals. Educators pool their resources and knowledge to engage in shared decision making toward a common goal. It is a way to accomplish a goal that may not be attainable alone (Bauer et al., 2010). As noted, this process is associated with improved student outcomes; however, it is not always easy for professionals to do. For one, some educators prefer to work alone—they may feel that others lack needed skills or that it is simply easier or faster to work alone.

When the benefits of interprofessional collaboration are clear and educators want to work together, another barrier can arise: the lack of time and resources to collaborate. Many teachers and related services providers have large caseloads, making it challenging to find time to focus on one student. Electronic collaboration strategies, such as web conferencing and cloud-based document management services, can be

Interprofessional collaboration allows teachers, who are being tasked with a wider range of responsibilities in today's schools, to rely on support from others to complete their responsibilities.

used to allow professionals to work in a collaborative way even when they may not have the time to meet together in person or at the same time (Charles & Dickens, 2012).

Roles and Responsibilities in the Inclusive Classroom

When instructional practices are identified through interprofessional collaboration, the next step in effective inclusive education is clearly defining the roles and responsibilities of the people providing instruction. This is because educators must leave their traditional silos of special classrooms, therapy rooms, or other separate spaces to support student learning in general education settings. To accomplish this, teaching itself will look different. Educators must work together in new ways to provide instruction to all students, including using new instructional strategies and groupings to meet the needs of all learners. For example, high school special and general educators may design lessons that are universally accessible to all students, including use of audio books, videos, and speech-to-text software, by drawing on their combined knowledge of the content and effective instructional practices. Educators will also likely engage in new activities, including coaching, consulting, and collaborating. Because co-teachers will likely have different skills and backgrounds (e.g., one is trained in to deliver special education services and another trained to teach biology), some degree of coaching may be necessary to support co-teachers in developing new instructional skills, classroom management skills, and other skills. Coaches work with other professionals (e.g., teachers, related services providers, paraprofessionals) to provide resources and strategies that can be used in the classroom. Coaches work directly with the other professionals, often completing observations followed by discussion and problem solving to support skill development and ultimately build their capacity to implement effective practices (Wlodarczyk et al., 2015). Likewise, consultation occurs when professionals meet together to discuss a student and offer advice. Using these strategies, educators work together to plan and problem solve, ensuring effective inclusive instruction is provided.

Inclusive education also requires a rethinking in how paraprofessionals are employed to support students with disabilities. Traditionally, paraprofessionals work one to one with students, assuming a primarily teaching role. Consequences of this use of paraprofessionals include lack of teacher involvement in instruction, student dependency on adult support, and barriers to peers and other natural supports, among others (e.g., Giangreco & Broer, 2005). An alternative to reliance on one-to-one paraprofessionals in the inclusive classroom is use of class-wide paraprofessionals. These paraprofessionals are assigned to classrooms rather than students. For example, a paraprofessional may be assigned to third-period biology, in which a small number of students receiving special education services are enrolled (in natural proportions). The paraprofessionals in such a classroom setting are a support for all students; rather than being assigned to specific students, they instead circulate around the room, providing cues, prompts, reminders, and assistance as needed. They will, of course, be particularly available for students with disabilities or other students who may need more support. This support arrangement is associated with many benefits to students and teachers: it facilitates more teacher time with individual students by reducing the teacher-to-student ratio, decreases stigmatization and dependency on adult supports, allows students more opportunities to respond and get feedback from an educator, and facilitates peer interactions.

Peer-assisted learning is yet another opportunity to provide effective instruction in the inclusive classroom. Peer-assisted learning occurs when same-age peers partner with a student with a disability and provide supports for their partner to learn and participate (Carter, 2017). For example, a peer partner might prompt a student to use a speech-generating device, model how to respond to a question, or work with together on an assignment, among many other possible supports. Peers are excellent support providers in inclusive classrooms for several reasons: (a) they know what matters in the social environment of the school and can help students with disabilities navigate these expectations and provide social opportunities; (b) working with a peer is far less stigmatizing than working with an adult—often, adult supports are real barriers to peer interactions; (c) peer supports are readily available and therefore a good support solution to schools that lack other resources; and (d) peer partners benefit academically, socially, and behaviorally from these partnerships (Carter, 2017). Ideal peer partners have good school attendance and are the preferred partners of students with disabilities; in other words, although adults often create these partnerships, the preferences of the student with disabilities should be sought and included in any partnership decisions.

Considering the variety of new roles and responsibilities in inclusive classrooms, including when peer supports are used, it is essential to clearly describe the expectations of all adults. To clarify the new roles and responsibilities of all educators and peer partners in the inclusive classroom, a co-teaching roles and responsibilities plan can be useful. Table 3.2 offers a template for creating such a plan, inviting educators to identify the major routines of a lesson, the co-teaching and other responsibilities of the general education teacher, the co-teaching and other responsibilities of the special education teacher, the activities of the paraprofessional, and the responsibilities of the peer partner. Also note that this overall plan includes planning prior to instruction, as well as reflection at the end of the lesson. Several of the planning aspects offered in Table 3.3 are discussed in the following sections.

Teaching Strategies in Inclusive Classrooms

In addition to considering the instructional arrangements of inclusive classroom, we now describe the process of teaching students with disabilities in inclusive settings. We consider three key processes: instructional cycles, inclusive schedules, and inclusive instructional plans.

Instructional Cycles

Effective instructional cycles include three components: co-planning, co-teaching, and progress monitoring. As shown in Figure 3.1, this is an iterative process, with each step continuously informing the next.

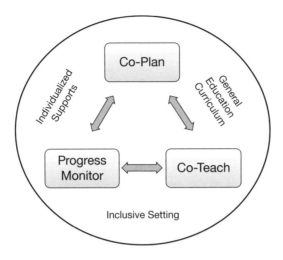

FIGURE 3.1 Instructional Cycle for Inclusive Education

Co-planning

Special and general educators must work together to plan for instructional content, supports, and assessment and be prepared to plan and implement a variety of strategies to ensure the progress and participation of each student. Co-planning is a means of accomplishing these goals and thus should occur regularly, preferably at the start of each unit of study. When co-planning, educators should find a distraction-free time (i.e., not during instruction or otherwise supervising students) when they will have curricular materials available to discuss (Murawski, 2012).

Educators should identify the routine components of each lesson (e.g., lecture, small group work, labs) and identify how instruction will be provided,

Special and general educators must work together to plan for instructional content, supports, and assessment and be prepared to plan and implement a variety of strategies to ensure the progress and participation of each student.

what content will be covered, who will provide instruction, and how student supports will be delivered (Toews et al., 2020). Planning for a unit of study is more efficient than planning for each lesson, by allowing educators to focus on how they will teach and provide supports during routine activities; thus, identifying those routine activities and developing plans for them prevent the need for detailed planning on a daily basis.

TABLE 3.3 Inclusive Instruction Roles and Responsibilities Template: Circle Critical Elements for Each Routine Activity for Each Application

ROUTINE ACTIVITIES	GENERAL EDUCATION TEACHER RESPONSIBILITIES	SPECIAL EDUCATION TEACHER RESPONSIBILITIES	PARAPROFESSIONAL RESPONSIBILITIES	PEER PARTNER RESPONSIBILITIES
Planning (prior to instruction)	• Develop lesson plans • Determine needed materials • Align lessons with standards, IEPs • Plan groupings and activities • Identify accommodations, modifications, and supports	• Develop lesson plans • Determine needed materials • Align lessons with standards, IEPs • Plan groupings and activities • Identify accommodations, modifications, and supports	• Prepare accommodations and modifications per teacher direction • Obtain needed materials • Assist in coordinating and managing activities	• Not applicable
Whole group	• One teach, one support • Team teaching • Parallel teaching • Station teaching • Alternative teaching • Individual instruction • Other:	• One teach, one support • Team teaching • Parallel teaching • Station teaching • Alternative teaching • Individual instruction • Other:	• Not present • Class-wide supports • Individual supports • Data collection • Clerical • Support peer partner • Other:	• Not present • Social/friendship supports • Academic supports • Communication supports • Other

Small group (labs, stations, centers)	• One teach, one support • Team teaching • Parallel teaching • Station teaching • Alternative teaching • Other:	• One teach, one support • Team teaching • Parallel teaching • Station teaching • Alternative teaching • Individual instruction • Other:	• Not present • Class-wide supports • Individual supports • Data collection • Clerical • Support peer partner • Other:	• Not present • Social/friendship supports • Academic supports • Communication supports • Other
Independent work	• One teach, one support • Team teaching • Parallel teaching • Station teaching • Alternative teaching • Other:	• One teach, one support • Team teaching • Parallel teaching • Station teaching • Alternative teaching • Individual instruction • Other:	• Not present • Class-wide supports • Individual supports • Data collection • Clerical • Support peer partner • Other:	• Not present • Social/friendship supports • Academic supports • Communication supports • Other
After the lesson	• Review student data • Review student accommodations, modifications, and supports • Review groupings • Grading	• Review student data • Review student accommodations, modifications, and supports • Review groupings • Grading	• Compile student data • Assist in reviewing accommodations, modifications, and supports • Assist in review of groupings • Assist in grading	• Not applicable

Co-teaching

A significant benefit of inclusive instruction is the possibility of using co-teaching arrangements, in which two or more adults work together to provide instruction to students (Friend et al., 2010). As noted by Murawski (2012), a variety of co-teaching arrangements are possible (listed in Table 3.2): (a) one teach, one support, when one educator is providing instruction to the whole class, while the other educator provides support (e.g., setting up labs, classroom management, data collection); (b) team teaching, in which both teachers provide instruction (e.g., taking turns, modeling how to solve a problem); (c) parallel teaching, in which one educator provides instruction to one half of the class while the other educator provides education to the other half of the class at the same time; (d) station teaching, in which students rotate among different stations or centers, with an educator at different stations; and (e) alternative teaching, in which one educator works with a large group of students while the other educator works with a small group of students. Educators may use different co-teaching arrangements on different days, different lessons within a day, or different activities within a lesson. In other words, educators can decide what sort of co-teaching arrangement will work best for them, given their unique interests, skill sets, and preferences.

Progress Monitoring

Successful educators collect formative data to measure the effectiveness of their instruction. Educators will draw on these data to make instructional decisions. For example, a kindergarten teacher may collect progress monitoring data on how accurately students rhyme words, and use data to decide which students need to be provided more intensive instruction. This continuous process of instruction,

In the inclusive setting, general and special educators work together to collect data, analyze data, and make instructional decisions with this information.

assessment, and data-based decision making is used to ensure adequate student progress in the general education curriculum (Watson et al., 2011). In the inclusive setting, general and special educators work together to collect data, analyze data, and make instructional decisions with this information. As such, these roles and responsibilities should be defined during the collaborative planning time.

Designing Effective Inclusive Supports

Inclusive Schedules

Creating schedules that make supports available, when needed, in inclusive settings is essential to ensuring student progress. This requires an integration of teacher, student, support staff and related services providers schedules. Considering the number of factors to include in the schedule for a single student, the task of designing schedules for a caseload of students becomes quite complex! Generally speaking, then, it is recommended that educators work together to design schedules for students that maximize available resources.

To start, consider the routines that the general education classroom students will participate in, and work with educators to make sure that instructional times when students need support are staggered. In a case study of an effective elementary school, McLeskey et al. (2014) found that teachers provided instruction in core areas (e.g., literacy) at different times of the day, enabling co-teachers and other support staff to be present. Without this simple planning activity, it is quite possible all elementary teachers would teach literacy, for example, at the same time, making it impossible for special educators to be present during literacy instruction in all classrooms.

With this master schedule of general education routines in place, the next step is layering in adult supports. Educators should identify when to co-plan, when to co-teach, and which class activities will have supports of a class-wide paraprofessional. In doing so, adult supports are provided when needed, while other natural supports (e.g., peer-assisted learning) are available for other instructional routines.

Finally, work with related services providers (e.g., speech and language pathologists) to decide on appropriate times and manners for the delivery of these supports. These supports may also include co-teaching; for example, a speech language pathologist may provide small group instruction during a small group activity to teach social communication skills. Other times, the related services provider may need to provide direct instruction in a separate setting due to the nature of the service. However, because pull-out services disrupt learning and account for hours of lost instructional time transitioning to separate areas and missing ongoing instruction, they should be minimized and carefully planned.

Inclusive Instructional Plans

Upon completion of schedules, the next crucial step in delivering effective inclusive instruction is planning what to teach and when to teach it.

What to Teach. What to teach would be based on the general education curriculum and student IEP goals. While this may seem rather straightforward, educators are often challenged to find ways to help students with disabilities "keep up" in both the general education and all IEP goals. Thus, we offer two tips:

- *Ensure IEP goals are linked to grade-appropriate state standards as much as possible.* This will prevent IEP goals from competing with standards for time and instruction. A variety of strategies exist for relating IEP goals to standards, including ensuring that (a) the student's grade level is the point of reference and (b) the goals have centrality with the content and performance expectations of the standard (Browder et al., 2006).
- *Prioritize learning as part of a data-based, team decision-making process.* A critical goal of education is that students keep learning. Often, however, we become overly focused on keeping up. Thus, educators must make decisions that ensure students keep learning, even if they do not keep up with the pace of instruction in the general education classroom. One option is to work with the student's team to prioritize learning content for each unit of instruction (Giangreco et al., 2011). For example, a high school biology class may learn 50 vocabulary words and another 20 key concepts in a unit of study focused on cell meiosis and mitosis. For some students, this is the appropriate number of words and concepts to learn. Other students should learn a different number of concepts. Perhaps a student with significant cognitive disability will learn five vocabulary words and two concepts. The team will decide which of those words and concepts have the most relevance to the student and ensure that curricular adaptations and supports focus on those words and concepts. This allows the student to keep learning grade-aligned academic content, without the pressure of keeping up. As students receive

instruction and educators collect data, teams can adjust the curricular goals for a student during a lesson based on rate of learning, as needed.

When to Teach. With grade-aligned IEP goals developed and instructional goals identified for a unit of study, educators can then address the next concern: when to teach. Far too often, when to teach has been conflated with where to teach. That is, often students have goals that differ substantially from what is taught in general education, and teams have no clear instructional goals for learning general education content. As a result, students are pulled out of general education classrooms and taught skills in special education settings.

This is avoidable not only by using the strategies discussed previously but also by using embedded instruction, in an evidenced-based practice (Jimenez & Kamei, 2015) that involves overlaying general education routines with student IEP goals and instructional priorities. Teams determine when, in a typical day, students will have natural opportunities to practice IEP goals and instructional priorities. They then determine if students have enough opportunities to practice skills in a typical day. If not enough opportunities are present (based on student progress monitoring data), additional supplemental opportunities are provided. For example, math is a natural time to work on addition and subtraction IEP goals, and small-group work is a natural time to work on social communication goals.

The instructional priorities identified for general education classes will have many natural opportunities to practice them during most class days. However, some students have IEP goals that are necessary for a student but may not occur often enough during a typical school day. For example, perhaps a high school student with significant cognitive disability is learning to identify coins by name and value. Because most high school students have mastered this skill, it is not taught in high school courses. The only natural times to practice coins would be in the school snack bar, but this still presents too few opportunities. The team could then embed supplemental teaching opportunities for coin identification during noninstructional moments throughout the day, including while the teacher is taking attendance, when students are getting out materials, or transitioning between activities. During these times, a peer partner, paraprofessional, or teacher could present an instructional opportunity (e.g., "which one is five cents?" while holding two coins). This could be repeated a few times throughout the day, enabling students to practice a variety of skills (McDonnell et al., 2008) without having to leave the general education classroom or miss instruction to practice learning priority skills.

Technology in Inclusive Classrooms

Personal technology today is ubiquitous: smartphones, tablets, and voice assistants in our homes that can do everything from answer questions to turn on lights—in short, technology has a profound impact on daily life today. This same technology is also transforming how we provide instruction. Students have access to supports such as speech-to-text software, screen-reading programs, voice-output communication devices, and many others in ways unheard of just a few years ago. As these technologies gain users and simplify life for people around the world, their cost continues to decrease, and their availability in schools spreads. It is essential that students with and without disabilities have access to and opportunities to learn with these technologies, as appropriate, not only to prepare them to be citizens of the world today but also to facilitate learning.

Universal Design for Learning

Like any personalized support, students are not born knowing what technology suits them best, or how to use technology. Instruction and opportunity must therefore be provided to students on a regular basis, enabling them to learn what works best for them and choose to use specific technologies for specific purposes. Inclusive educators must embed technology in their classrooms, using strategies such as universal design for learning (UDL; Cook & Rao, 2018). As discussed in Chapter 2, UDL is based on the prem-

UDL is based on the premise that all instruction should be designed from the beginning to reduce barriers.

ise that all instruction should be designed from the beginning to reduce barriers, and technology provides ready means of reducing barriers. For example, in a literacy class in which students are learning text comprehension through reading a novel, educators might provide several forms of the novel: in print form, in audio form via text-to-speech software, and simplified text enhanced with images.

Using a UDL approach, students choose which format they prefer to learn from and are held to the same text comprehension expectations regardless of form.

Technology-Assisted Learning

Technology is also useful in making learning fun and engaging. Often educators fear technology will be distracting to students, yet many students prefer to use technology to learn because they believe it makes learning more fun and interesting. Difficult or "boring" subjects can come to life through virtual lessons, videos, and interactive games. Importantly, technology-assisted learning (learning on tablets or computers) can also facilitate personalized learning. The use of these technologies reduces stigma and enables students to work on materials that are appropriate to their skill level using the supports they need (e.g., large font or text-to-speech). Technology can similarly enable students to learn at their own pace through this personalized instruction. Research has documented how various apps can be used to teach diverse skills, such as phonics to students who use speech-generating applications on iPads (Ahlgrim-Delzell et al., 2016) and writing for students with cognitive disability (Felix et al., 2017). In sum, integration of technology in the inclusive classroom has the capacity of technology to open doors for student learning, communicating, and personalized supports in ways that were impossible in previous generations.

Conclusion

In this chapter we have taken a necessarily broad look at answering the question, How can we teach better? These effective practices emerged from second-generation inclusive practices (discussed in greater detail in Chapter 5) in which students with disabilities were increasingly being included in the general education classroom, and teachers needed to know how to teach them in that context. Each practice could be a book in and of itself, and future volumes of the Norton Inclusive Education for Students With Disabilities series will expand on some of these. It is important to understand that evidence-based and high-leverage practices have been shown to be important to inclusive education.

Reflective Questions for Group Study

1. How do family-school partnerships, instructional strategies, teaching arrangements, teaching strategies, and technology each raise expectations and promote positive student outcomes?

2. In what ways do educator roles and responsibilities change in an inclusive classroom?

3. How do the instructional cycles described in this chapter create an opportunity for continuous evaluation and improvement of inclusive instruction?

4. Describe how application of the Universal Design for Learning framework would improve inclusive opportunities for all students.

4

How Do We Know It's Working?

Evidence in Support of Inclusive Education

There is an increased focus on educating students with disabilities in inclusive general education settings due to converging policy guidelines, ethics, and research-based evidence over the past several decades. As discussed in Chapter 1, the 2004 Individuals With Disabilities Education Act (IDEA) and the 2015 Every Student Succeeds Act focus on students learning the general education curriculum, in the general education setting. Moreover, IDEA requires schools to provide students with disabilities "access to the general education curriculum . . . to learn grade-level content based on grade-level standards" (§300.26(b)(3)(ii)), whereby the state standards determine the core curriculum.

In addition to policy reasons, inclusive education is supported by ethical considerations. One key ethical rationale is that disability is simply part of human diversity and the human experience. This view of disability encompasses acceptance and respect. It also highlights that, for a community to embrace and celebrate the diversity within each person, we must learn together and from one another to know and appreciate one another and move beyond simply tolerance of one another. Inclusive education, as such, is fundamental to achieving and celebrating diversity, as it advocates that students learn together in schools to prepare them to live and work together throughout life.

A growing and substantial body of research supports inclusive education; in fact, the past 40 years of research shows that, when students with and without disabilities learn together, they experience better outcomes. A key benefit of inclusive settings is the presence of the general education teacher, who has expertise in the core academic content, along with materials and tools for teaching that content (Kleinert et al., 2015). Inclusive education also has been shown to improve the ability of teachers to provide quality instruction to all students, including students with disabilities (Finke et al., 2009). Other benefits of inclusive education for students with disabilities include improvements to quality of life and enhanced educational experiences (Hunt et al., 2012). Research further suggests inclusive education contributes to improved postschool outcomes for students with disabilities (Mazzotti et al., 2013; Test et al., 2009).

This chapter focuses on describing the research evidence supporting inclusive education across five domains: academic, social-emotional learning, communication, friendships and relationships, and the impact on nondisabled students. We then consider how these data compel us to make changes within schools to provide opportunities for people with disabilities to experience positive outcomes across the life span. We consider two groups of students with disabilities: (a) Students with "high-incidence" disabilities comprise the majority of students with disabilities, which include students with learning disabilities, attention deficit disorders, and speech and language impairments, among others; (b) Students with "low-incidence disabilities" comprise about 1% of students who have significant cognitive disability and are eligible to take their state's alternate assessment.

Academic Progress

Educational research indicates that increased academic competency for *all* students in the areas of literacy, math, and science is associated with improved future outcomes. For example, literacy skills lead to substantially improved opportunities for educational, economic, and overall life outcomes. In the area of mathematics, even the most basic knowledge of math skills increases employability prospects later in life. Competency in higher-level math

> *Increased academic competency for all students in the areas of literacy, math, and science is associated with improved future outcomes.*

skills leads to additional postsecondary educational opportunities, a variety of potential career options, and increased economic success (Wei et al., 2012).

Clearly, academic achievement matters and should be considered when developing individualized education programs (IEPs) for students with disabilities, and when determining where those IEP services are provided. A large and growing body of research demonstrates that students with disabilities learn academic skills equally, if not better, in inclusive settings compared to self-contained special education classrooms. We first consider students with high-incidence disabilities. Several studies have directly compared outcomes for students with high-incidence disabilities taught in inclusive settings versus students taught in separate special education or resource classrooms. For example, Tremblay (2013) compared the reading and writing scores of students with learning disabilities taught in inclusive versus self-contained classrooms and found students in inclusive classrooms obtained higher scores. Similarly, Cole et al. (2020) compared the state assessment reading and math scores of nearly 1,700 students in fourth through eighth grade with high-incidence disabilities. Students with disabilities who spent more time in general education settings did significantly better in both math and reading assessments than did students who spent more time in separate special education classrooms.

A similar pattern of academic benefit is present for students with low-incidence disabilities. For example, Dessemontet et al. (2012) investigated the literacy and math outcomes of 68 children with intellectual disability: 34 were taught in an inclusive school, and 34 were taught in separate special education classrooms. The students in the inclusive classroom had better literacy skills, and there was no difference in math outcomes. Kurth and Mastergeorge (2010) reviewed the educational progress of 15 students with autism and intellectual disability, whose educational records were reviewed from kindergarten through ninth grade.

> *Students with disabilities learn academic skills equally, if not better, in inclusive settings compared to self-contained special education classrooms.*

The students had been continuously enrolled in either an inclusive school or separate special education classroom for 10 years (K-9). The researchers found those students who had been taught in inclusive classrooms obtained significantly higher reading, math, and writing outcomes than their matched peers in self-contained programs.

Social-Emotional Learning

Often, students with disabilities are removed from general education classrooms because they engage in problem behaviors. Sometimes students struggle to learn because of unmet social-emotional needs, thus putting them at risk for removal to remedial special education programs or classrooms dedicated to teaching students with emotional-behavioral disorders. Other times, teachers have difficulty connecting with students who have problem behaviors or who are withdrawn, resulting in students falling behind and being referred for special education services. Clearly, social, emotional, and behavioral outcomes are important to helping students learn and thrive at school. Research has demonstrated students have more positive social-emotional trajectories into adulthood, engaging in fewer antisocial behaviors, when they are taught in inclusive settings (Woodman et al., 2016). This research suggests that removal of students due to problem behavior is counterproductive, and students should be taught emotional regulation skills in context. In other words, students should be taught coping strategies and/or replacement behaviors in the natural setting, when and where those skills are needed.

One strategy for teaching social-emotional skills in the inclusive context is using peer-assisted learning; this has been found to be highly effective in promoting positive social-emotional outcomes for students with and at risk for experiencing disability (Moeyaert et al., 2019). Another consideration related to social-emotional learning is related to student self-sufficiency and independence, which includes such skills as being able to do tasks independently. A longitudinal study found that students with disabilities taught in inclusive settings demonstrated more independence and self-sufficiency than did students who were taught in self-contained special education classes (Newman & Davies-Mercier, 2005). Students taught in inclusive settings demonstrate better self-determination skills overall (Hughes et al., 2013). Finally, researchers have found that adolescents with disabilities taught in inclusive settings are more engaged in curricular activities than their peers who are taught in self-contained settings (Kurth & Mastergeorge, 2012). Together, these research studies demonstrate that inclusive education is strongly associated with a variety of positive social-emotional outcomes for students with disabilities.

> *Students have more positive social-emotional trajectories into adulthood, engaging in fewer antisocial behaviors, when they are taught in inclusive settings.*

Communication

Communication is at the core of the school experience, as it is necessary to engage in academic learning with teachers and to socialize with peers. In fact, communication is used throughout the day for nearly every activity, both as children and later as adults. For those reasons, communication is frequently mentioned as a critical personalized education skill. But for students with disabilities who have complex communication needs—students who need supports to communicate effectively—this experience is compromised when communication needs are not addressed. Students with complex communication needs may use such supports as pictures or text to supplement their voice, whereas some students communicate with augmentative and alternative communication, such as speech-generating devices. Students with disabilities who have complex communication needs are at risk of not gaining access to the general education curriculum, obtaining poor academic outcomes, not being placed in the general education classroom, and experiencing low expectations from school personnel (Kurth et al., 2014; Kleinert et al., 2015; Ruppar et al., 2011).

Just as students with disabilities who demonstrate problem behaviors are more likely to be taught in self-contained settings, so too are students with disabilities who have communication support needs. Although far too many students with complex communication needs leave school without an effective means of communicating, inclusive education has been shown to improve communication outcomes (Foreman et al., 2016). One reason for this is that inclusive settings are far more likely to contain communication partners. Within self-contained classrooms, many students have complex communication needs, leaving fewer competent communication partners with whom to practice and develop social communication skills. Inclusive settings also contain more students, meaning there are better chances of finding peers with similar interests with whom to communicate. Finally, the discourse of inclusive classrooms (the language students are exposed to) has been found to be much richer, giving students more opportunities to hear varied language structures and develop communication skills.

Friendships and Relationships

Ask anyone what they most remember about their time in school, and invariably they think about the social activities they enjoyed with friends, either at recess in elementary school or in sports, clubs, or other after school events in secondary school. Forming friendships and relationships is crucial to development and, frankly, for many results in some of the most enjoyable aspects of school and work. Given the importance of social relationships, friendship and relationship outcomes of inclusive education have been extensively researched. This research has consistently found that students with disabilities taught in inclusive settings have better social skills and more robust social networks than do students with disabilities taught in separate classrooms (Fisher & Meyer, 2002).

Researchers have suggested that students with disabilities have greater growth in social skills when they are taught in inclusive settings, largely as a result of access to social networks and peer models (McDonnell et al., 2002). In fact, students

> *Students with disabilities taught in inclusive settings have better social skills and more robust social networks than do students with disabilities taught in separate classrooms.*

with disabilities taught in inclusive settings have larger social networks and more opportunities to develop social skills (Kennedy & Itkonen, 2016). Students with disabilities taught in inclusive settings have higher levels of social engagement (Lyons et al., 2011).

Impact on Students Without Disabilities

So far in this chapter we have focused on students with disabilities; this research has highlighted the many benefits of inclusive education for students with disabilities. However, many teachers, parents, and administrators are concerned about the impact of inclusive education on students without disabilities. What do we know about the outcomes of inclusive education for students who do not have a disability? Luckily, a large body of research dedicated to this question has demonstrated that educating students with disabilities within the general education classroom does not harm

> *Educating students with disabilities within the general education classroom does not harm students without disabilities and may benefit them.*

students without disabilities and may benefit them. In 2007 researchers systematically reviewed 26 different studies focusing on the impact of inclusive education on the academic development of students without disabilities, finding that 81% of study outcomes reported students without disabilities either experienced no effects or experienced positive effects (Kalambouka et al., 2007). A similar review completed in 2009 came to the same conclusion: inclusive education of students with disabilities has either a positive or neutral impact on the academic outcomes of students without disabilities (Ruijs & Peetsma, 2009).

Why might inclusive education have either a positive or neutral impact on learners without disabilities? Several reasons are possible. First, teachers in inclusive classrooms are likely to adapt how they teach to benefit all students, including the use of strategies and techniques that meet the needs of diverse learners (Dessemontet & Bless, 2013). Second, teachers working in inclusive settings may collaborate more, gathering strategies and supports from colleagues in ways that benefit all students (Sharma et al., 2008). Third, coordinated schoolwide approaches to positive behavior support and multitiered systems of supports may also equip teachers with strategies to meet the behavior and learning needs of all students through a collaborative, interdisciplinary problem-solving approach (Giangreco et al., 1993).

Examining Trends in Placement

Research spanning several decades demonstrates students with and without disabilities benefit from an inclusive education, which also supports effective teaching. We also note that, when asked, parents and families tend to support an inclusive education, believing it benefits their children academically and socially (Peck et al., 2004). Considering that IDEA requires education teams to make educational decisions based on research, it is clear the research supports inclusive education, and this should therefore be the de facto placement for students with disabilities who receive special education services in the United States. In short, we are out of excuses *not* to include students with disabilities. There is no compelling reason for segregation and separation for part or all of the school day.

However, review of data reported by states on the implementation of IDEA, which includes where students with disabilities receive special education services, reveals limited progress in teaching all students with disabilities in the inclusive setting. According to the most recent report to Congress on the implementation of IDEA (Office of Special Education and Rehabilitative Services, 2019), only 63.5% of students with disabilities are included in general education settings; 18.1% were taught in resource settings (part of the day in general education and part of the day in separate classrooms), 13.3% were taught mostly in separate self-contained classrooms, and 5% were taught in entirely separate schools. A closer look at these data reveal troubling trends: little progress has been made in educating more students with disabilities in inclusive settings, and students with high-incidence disabilities are much more likely to be included in general education compared to students with low-incidence disabilities.

In considering progress in educating more students with disabilities in inclusive settings, McLeskey et al. (2012) tracked student placement between the 1990–1991 school year and the 2007–2008 school year. They found that approximately 39% of students with disabilities were taught in inclusive settings in the 1990–1991 school year, and 65.5% were taught in this placement by the 2007–2008 school year. However, most of this increasing placement in inclusive settings came from students with high-incidence disabilities, specifically students with learning disabilities and speech language impairments. Students with emotional-behavioral disorders experienced very little change. Morningstar, Kurth, and colleagues (2017) completed a similar review focused on students with low-incidence disabilities, examining placement trends between 2000 and 2014 for students with autism, intellectual disability, multiple disability, and deaf-blindness. They found that this group of students is about four times more likely to be taught in separate self-contained classrooms than in general education inclusive settings, representing almost no change between 2000 and 2014.

Pulling It All Together

As we have established in this chapter, placement matters for student outcomes within school. Emerging research also demonstrates that school placement has lifelong consequences. Unfortunately, students with disabilities are at risk for absenteeism and grade retention, as well as not graduating from high school, which has numerous consequences, including poor economic outcomes and increased risk for experiencing lifelong poor health outcomes (Yoder & Cantrell, 2019). The most recent report to Congress on the implementation of IDEA found that, among students with disabilities between the ages of 14 and 21, approximately

15% dropped out of school, only 45% graduated with a high school diploma, and only 2% received a certificate of completion (Office of Special Education and Rehabilitative Services, 2019). Among 18- to 24-year-olds, the dropout rate for people with disabilities is 15.2%, compared to 6.4% for people without disabilities. In fact, people with disabilities are more likely to drop out of school than any other group (National Center for Education Statistics, 2020).

Employment data offer equally bleak outcomes (Sannicandro et al., 2018), with rates of employment for persons with disabilities remaining static at around 34% (Smith et al., 2017). Eighty-one percent of adults with disabilities received segregated services in day habilitation, clinic, rehabilitation, or other segregated day programs as adults (Braddock et al., 2015). Because the Fair Labor Standards Act (29 CFR §14(c)) allows employers to pay workers with disabilities subminimum wages, earnings of employees in sheltered workshops and other segregated settings are significantly reduced (Kregel & Dean, 2002). Of all participants in total day or work programs, only 19% worked in supported employment (Braddock et al., 2015), which substantially increases earnings of workers (Wehman et al., 2018).

Young adults with low-incidence disabilities experience the poorest postsecondary outcomes of any disability group (Newman et al., 2011). Students with low-incidence disabilities continue to exit school without the skills they need to be successful (Kearns et al., 2010). Many students have inadequate communication supports available by the time they leave school (Erickson & Geist, 2016; Kleinert et al., 2015), which can substantially impact postschool employment, social, and recreational opportunities. Limited social skills and lowered expectations are associated with diminished postschool employment outcomes (Carter et al., 2012). For people with low-incidence disabilities, an equally concerning postschool outcome is related to integrated community living. Although people with low-incidence disabilities report preferring to live in apartments with support (Ioanna, 2018), nearly 71% lived with a family or caregiver, and only 16% lived alone or with a roommate in the community (Braddock et al., 2015).

> Students with disabilities who had received special education services in inclusive general education settings were more likely to obtain postsecondary education, be employed, and live independently as adults.

Together, these findings demonstrate a systemic failure of the current model of teaching students with disabilities (Morningstar, Zagona, et al., 2017). Reviewing the outcomes of special education (e.g., employment, independent living, postsecondary education) clearly demonstrates that the status quo of teaching remedial skills in special education classrooms has never led to positive outcomes for students with disabilities once they leave school. We are thus compelled to do better; we must make changes in schools to better prepare for students for life after school, and this includes educating students in general education classrooms, with the supports they need, to learn the general education curriculum. Preliminary data supports this: students with disabilities who had received special education services in inclusive general education settings were more likely to obtain postsecondary education, be employed, and live independently as adults (Mazzotti et al., 2016; Test et al., 2009).

In summary, the research we have reviewed in this chapter demonstrates that students with disabilities have better outcomes in school when taught in inclusive classrooms. They are more likely to achieve important academic, social, emotional, behavioral, communication, and relationship outcomes when taught alongside their peers without disabilities. Students taught in inclusive settings during their school years also achieved more positive postschool outcomes as adults, including rates of employment, postsecondary education, and independent living. Finally, students without disabilities experienced no negative consequences from being taught in classrooms that included students with disabilities. Thus, these data offer compelling reasons to teach all students, including those with disabilities, the general education curriculum in inclusive settings.

Reflective Questions for Group Study

1. Summarize the research around inclusive education for students with and without disabilities.
2. Describe the extent to which students with high- and low-incidence disabilities learn in inclusive settings, and any notable trends in their placement over time.
3. How does school placement in inclusive or special classes impact long-term outcomes?
4. Is our current model of educating students effective in promoting positive lifelong outcomes? Why or why not?

5

Where Do We Go From Here?

The Fourth Generation of Inclusive Education

In previous chapters we asked and tried to answer questions about who we teach, how we teach, what principles drive our teaching, what practices work, and how we know that inclusive practices are effective. Now, we want to pull together some of the elements we have discussed in previous chapters and ask, Where do we go from here? What does inclusive education look like as we move forward? Before we do that, let us consider how inclusive education has been conceptualized to up to this point.

First, the emphasis in promoting inclusion has principally focused on students in classrooms. That is logical, of course, given the history of the field of special education. Turnbull et al. (2010) characterized the growth of the inclusive education movement as unfolding in three generations of practice. In the *first generation*, a push against the de facto segregation that came in with the 1975 passage of the Education for All Handicapped Children Act, as discussed in Chapter 1. The first generation of inclusive practices focused on getting students physically into classrooms with their nondisabled peers. Once some students were receiving their education within regular education environments with their nondisabled peers, there was a need to figure out how to teach those students in those inclusive settings. That *second generation* of inclusive practices developed and refined the practices discussed in Chapter 3.

With the passage of the 1997 reauthorization of Individuals With Disabilities Education Act (IDEA), discussed in Chapter 2, a *third generation* of inclusive

practices emerged: what was required pertained not only to the "where" of educating students but also to the "what" of educating students. Just being in the
classroom was no longer sufficient; IDEA required that students receiving special
education needed to be involved with and progress in the same curriculum as did
their peers without disabilities. These generations of practice have one thing in
common: they focused on individual students in individual classrooms.

But the confluence of changes in education in personalized education today,
the movement away from standardized education toward personalized education, the changing paradigm for understanding disability, and the U.S. Supreme
Court's *Endrew F.* ruling—all discussed in Chapter 1—may be leading us to a
fourth generation of inclusive practices. In this chapter we lay out some of the foun-
dational components for building that fourth generation of inclusive education
for all learners.

Before doing that, however, we want to make this point: incrementalism as a
policy to achieve inclusive education has failed (Slee, 2001). In the realm of public
policy, *incrementalism* refers to the process of creating change through small, dis-
crete steps, as opposed to large jumps. Efforts to reform education and to implement inclusive education have been incremental: a pilot project here, changes in
the language in existing laws there, implementing a federally funded initiative
via a large project, and so forth. And, as we have discussed previously, the actual
changes in the daily lives for students and their families have been minimal. This
is not the time for tinkering around the edges of education. The field itself is
undergoing significant and lasting changes, which allows those of us concerned
about the education of students with disabilities to go beyond incrementalism
and to attempt to create systems that support all learners to be successful.

Inclusive Education Is Strengths Based

As a field we have limited ability to achieve the educational outcomes we desire
if we understand disability within a deficit model. More than 150 years of knowledge and practice has been predicated on deficits and pathology, and that has
taken us as far as it can (Wehmeyer, 2019). Whether we intend it or not, adhering
to a deficit-based perspective of disability perpetuates the purpose of special education as to "eradicate deficits to the greatest extent possible so that students . . .
function less atypically" (Thompson et al., 2010, p. 171). One is tempted to paraphrase the U.S. Supreme Court in its ruling in *Endrew F.*: "When all is said and

done, a student offered an educational program providing 'merely more than *de minimis*' progress from year to year can hardly be said to have been offered an education at all" (137 S. Ct. 988 [2017]). We would paraphrase this to state that, when special education is driven by a deficit model, when all is said and done, students offered educational programs intended to enable them to function less atypically can hardly be said to have been offered an education at all.

Inclusive education today must be built on foundations of strengths-based approaches that are derived from social and social-ecological models of disability and that shift the focus of education to identifying supports that enable students to be successful. We are not saying that there is no value to understanding the underlying neurological, physical, or anatomical reasons that result in disability. As Wehmeyer (2019) noted, there is utility in knowing that children with Down syndrome mature in their motor skills at a delayed rate and in understanding the areas of the brain involved with dyslexia, which allows us to design interventions and supports to bridge the gaps between what students can do and the demands of the environment or context in which they want to live, learn, work, or play. But we cannot start from the impairment; instead, we need to begin with a thorough understanding of what each student does well, what that student is passionate about and values, and what is meaningful to that student. We build our educational interventions around those factors and not around factors pertaining to deficits.

> *Inclusive education today must be built on foundations of strengths-based approaches that are derived from social and social-ecological models of disability and that shift the focus of education to identifying supports that enable students to be successful.*

Inclusive Education Emphasizes Supports

Throughout this book we have used the term *supports*, and indeed, the notion of supports is already inculcated into the language we use, such as in the terms *multitiered systems of supports* and *supplementary aids and supports*. In Chapter 1 we noted that historic models of special education have created programs to serve students with disability based on the type, intensity, or severity of the students' deficits. Strengths-based approaches to education emphasize individualized, personalized supports that account for students' preferences, interests, and abilities.

In the past two decades, considerable work has occurred in conceptualizing and operationalizing supports, and efforts to apply these innovations to education are now emerging (Thompson et al., 2010). Supports are, simply, resources and strategies that enhance personal functioning (Thompson et al. 2009). More specifically, *supports* refer to "resources and strategies that aim to promote the development, education, interests, and personal well-being of a person and that enhance individual functioning" (Luckasson et al., 2002, p. 151). Supports are, really, anything that enables a person to function successfully, participate in society, pursue meaningful goals, and live a self-determined life.

We all use supports in our day-to-day lives, from seeking advice from a friend on a topic of concern to GPS-enabled smartphones for navigating unfamiliar environments. Education itself is an important domain of supports, and within education myriad supports have been developed and shown to be effective in improving student learning, including peer supports, technology supports, adaptations and accommodations, curriculum design and modification, and more (Thompson et al., 2018). Supports are personalized, although specific types of

It becomes important to assess what supports are needed and to incorporate planning for the use of supports into the educational planning process.

supports may benefit a wide array of students, with and without disabilities. Still, not every student requires or will benefit from every support, so it becomes important to assess what supports are needed and to incorporate planning for the use of supports into the educational planning process.

Supports and Educational Planning

The individualized education program (IEP) process has become overly contentious and bureaucratic, and the impact of IEPs on meaningful educational outcomes for students with disabilities has been called into question (Thompson, 2016). In fields related to special education, such as career and vocational counseling, as efforts to implement personalized education roll out, the planning processes have begun to change to fit these changing contexts. This is happening incrementally in special education. The 1990 reauthorization of IDEA introduced requirements pertaining to planning for and delivering services to support a student's transition to adulthood. The requirements mandated that if such planning involved transition service, students had to be invited to the IEP meeting. This rather limited requirement, in concert with an initiative to promote student self-determination, led to the recognition that students benefit when they are involved in their educational planning (Wehmeyer & Sands, 1998; Williams-Diehm et al., 2008). The limitation to such efforts was that student-led planning and student involvement in educational planning were contextually linked to the disability-focused, increasingly bureaucratic IEP process.

Similarly, within the context of the education of learners with more intensive support needs, person-centered planning processes have been emphasized as important to soliciting input from a wide array of stakeholders and as a way to focus on student preferences and interests. There is ample evidence that, when done well, person-centered planning can result in educational plans that are strengths based and student focused. The problem has been that such processes take time, and in the context of teachers and administrators having back-to-back IEP meetings, it has been difficult to integrate person-centered planning into educational practices (Wehmeyer, 2002).

We need another model if we are to integrate supports and strengths-based planning into the educational process. Perhaps we can find such a model by looking at what is desired and required for all students, and not only students with disabilities. The 2015 Every Student Succeeds Act promotes the implementation of personalized learning by school districts. An important though too little empha-sized element of personal-ized learning is student voice and choice (National Center for Learning Dis-abilities, 2018).

> *When done well, person-centered planning can result in educational plans that are strengths based and student focused.*

There are several reasons that student choice and voice are not reliably emphasized in personalized learning. One is that there is skepticism that students will choose to learn what they "need" to learn. The U.S. Department of Education–funded Center on Innovations in Learning developed a handbook titled *Personalized Learning for States, Districts, and Schools* (Murphy et al., 2016) to assist local and state education agencies in implementing personalized education. In this handbook, Sota (2016) posed the question of how the positive impacts of learner choice and voice could be realized while minimizing the risk that students will not choose learning objectives that are in their best interest. Sota suggested that this can be achieved by designing models in which teachers and learners co-design instruction, with learners making choices coached by a teacher and informed by knowledge of current and desired skills. In this type of model, learners not only work on the knowledge and skills related to the instructional materials but also on self-regulated learning skills—learning how to learn. (p. 59)

In fact, we have models for the education of learners with disabilities (promoting self-determination and student involvement in educational planning) not only to focus on strengths-based supports planning but also for personalized learning planning for all students.

Solberg et al. (2018) have introduced the *individualized learning plan* (ILP) process, a form of a personalized learning plan that incorporates elements of support planning and planning for personalized learning that has been implemented widely with students with disabilities. The U.S. Department of Education (2017, p. 1) defines personalized learning plans "as a formalized process that involves . . . students setting learning goals based on personal, academic and career interests with the close support of school personnel or other individuals that can include teachers, school counselors, and parents." Currently, more than 40 states are implementing the ILP process (Solberg et al., 2018), which was developed and evaluated in the context of the life-designing process and can provide a useful model for planning for personalized education in inclusive contexts. A life design focus has emerged in the fields of career counseling and vocational guidance in response to the changing global economic context and the world of work. Savickas (2012, p. 13) captured the basic sense of the need for a life design approach, noting that "careers do not unfold; they are constructed as individuals make choices that express their self-concepts and substantiate their goals in the social reality of a work role."

> Students will need the skills and abilities to "design" their own lives, whether those designs are about work and careers, community inclusion, education and learning, or any other topic.

Further, Savickas et al. (2009) recognized that the life design approach was not just pertinent to young people transitioning into the world of work but, indeed, was applicable for all students in learning how to navigate personalized education and lifelong transitions. They proposed a life designing approach "framed as a lifelong self-construction process that aims to promote skills and competences in overall life planning" (Wehmeyer et al., 2019, p. 182). The gist is that students will need the skills and abilities to "design" their own lives, whether those designs are about work and careers, community inclusion, education and learning, or any other topic.

The ILP process, as detailed by the U.S. Department of Labor (Office of Disability Employment Policy, n.d.), involves three elements: self-exploration, career and planning management, and career exploration. Students identify any accommodations they might need to successfully implement their plans. Thompson et al. (2018) took this one step further to incorporate the identification of supplementary aids and services as part of the supports planning process for students and educators. You may recall from Chapter 1 that supplementary aids and services are defined in IDEA as "aids, services, and other supports that are provided in regular education classes, other education-related settings, and in extracurricular and nonacademic settings, to enable children with disabilities to be educated with nondisabled children to the maximum extent appropriate" (§300.42, https://sites.ed.gov/idea/regs/b/a/300.42). The Supports Intensity Scales can be used in the ILP process to provide children and adolescents a way to assess, in concert with the teacher and others, their areas of strengths and instructional needs and then use that information to identify what they need to successfully learn. As noted by Sota (2016), this does not mean that students are lone wolves in planning but are *co-designers* of education. We return to this theme when we discuss personalized and self-determined learning.

Inclusive Education Is Schoolwide

The first three generations of inclusive practice focused primarily on a student in a classroom. Sailor and Roger (2005) argued that, by placing the onus for inclusion primarily on teachers and by having the individual classroom as the primary focus for determining the success or failure of inclusion, we as a field have failed to take into account that teachers, students, and classrooms are part of a larger system within a school. Sailor and Roger suggested that the focus for promoting inclusive practices and for examining its impact should be at the school level. They identified six guiding principles and critical features of schoolwide models:

1. General education guides all student learning.
2. All school resources are configured to benefit all students.

3. Schools address social development and citizenship forthrightly.

4. Schools are democratically organized, data-driven, problem-solving systems.

5. Schools have open boundaries in relation to their families and communities.

6. Schools enjoy district support for understanding an extensive systems-change effort. (p. 506–508)

These principles overlay the principles of personalized learning (detailed below) in multiple areas.

In the 15 years since Sailor and Roger provided these principles, multiple schoolwide models have emerged that both shift the onus for inclusion from teachers and classrooms to the school as a system and, concurrently, adhere to social-ecological models of disability that focus on context and supports rather than deficits within the student. The most evident such practice involves multitiered systems of supports (MTSS). These systems evolved from the practices of response to intervention and of positive behavior interventions and supports (Wehmeyer, 2019), which are tiered-intervention models that focus on academic progress and on behavioral issues, respectively. But both share one more feature in addition to their tiered structures: they take a social-ecological model approach, focusing on modifying or changing the context and providing supports if students are having difficulty succeeding. And that focus carried over into MTSS.

As we discussed in Chapter 2, at the tier 1 level within MTSS, all students receive "high quality, evidence-based, and universally designed instruction, taking into consideration their linguistic and cultural backgrounds, disabilities, and other learning needs" (Shogren et al., 2016, p. 215). In historic models of schooling, if students are struggling to succeed, they are removed from general education classrooms and settings to receive specialized instruction, either for part of their school day or, too often, permanently. Within MTSS, consistent with social-ecological models of disability, what changes if students are not experiencing success is the context: students are provided different or more intensive levels of instruction to enable them to succeed. Importantly, as Shogren et al. (2016, p. 215) noted: "Students move to more intensive levels (tiers) of support, they do not need to be removed from general education classes. . . . Interventions can be embedded within general education instruction and activities, maintaining opportunities for the benefits of inclusion." It could be argued that schools that adopt MTSS must adopt inclusive practices. Maintaining segregated class-rooms is counter to the intent of MTSS. In a large-scale, federally funded technical assistance and training initiative, Sailor and colleagues (2018) developed and widely implemented a "reframed" version of inclusive schools, referred to as the Schoolwide Integrated Framework for Transformation, that builds school-wide systems to ensure that all students are included and receive equitable, high-quality instruction based on the backbone of an MTSS process.

Inclusive Education Emphasizes Personalized Learning

It seems clear, as we have emphasized this throughout this book, that inclusive education must align with emerging practices in personalized learning. Not only is this necessary to keep pace with innovation in education more broadly, but it is also fortuitous, since personalized learning adopts many of the principles and practices articulated for inclusive education. At the heart of personalized learning, as mentioned previously, is the student. Personalized learning is "an approach in which the instructional approach, outcomes, content, activities, pace, tools, and supports are customized for each individual learners' needs" (Basham et al., 2015, p. 10). What almost always takes center stage in discussions about personalized learning, however, is the "tools" element of this definition, specifically the role of technology in personalized learning. The National Center for Learning Disabilities (2018) conducted a comprehensive review of the literature in personalized learning and concluded that

> a theme that consistently emerged was that personalized learning requires students to make good choices about their learning, assert their needs and pursue their goals in order to be successful. These skill sets are vital for all learners, but they are especially important for students with disabilities. Yet these skills are not frequently taught to students, an omission that harms those who need these skills the most. (p. 2)

Although technology is an important part of achieving personalized learning and, indeed, inclusion, when the element of student choice and voice is missing, personalized learning is not likely to succeed. Zhao (2018) has forwarded four features of "personalizable education" as a means to refocus personalized learning on the student: agency, shared ownership, flexibility, and value creation.

Agency refers to being an actor in one's life, rather than being acted upon, and is closely aligned with the notion of self-determination, which we discuss further below. Zhao (2018, p. 58) stated that, "for students to explore, identify and enhance their strengths and follow their passions, they must become owners of their own learning. . . . They must have agency in designing their own learning." Going back to the ideas introduced by the life design process, it is clear that if students are to be able to construct and design their own lives, they need to learn the knowledge, skills, and attitudes that will enable them to be an agent in their own lives.

> At the heart of personalized learning is the student.

Shared ownership continues the theme emphasized by agency and picks up on the points Sota (2016) made about students and teachers being co-designers of education. Importantly, shared ownership not only empowers students but also empowers teachers. Far too often, teachers feel as disenfranchised in decisions about curriculum and instruction as do students. While the focus on agency is on the student, the focus of shared ownership is on learners and teachers, and cafeteria workers, counselors, and the myriad people who make up a school.

Flexibility is a defining feature of personalizable education, which must be able to respond "to new opportunities, emerging, needs, and unexpected problems" in "all aspects of the school: leadership, timetable, curriculum, facilities, students, and staffing" (Zhao, 2018, p. 64). Flexibility is first and foremost a mindset that "believes in the value of change and that plans, no matter how carefully thought out, will always have unexpected disruptions and/or outcomes that require change" (p. 64).

> Promoting self-determination is a critical element in life design and in promoting agency and shared ownership.

Flexibility is more than a mindset, however. It is critical to create learning communities and environments that foster agency and learning. Fullan et al. (2018, p. 14) argued that schools need to cultivate rich learning environments for children that are "driven by learner's curiosity, teach students to be problem designers, pose problems in which students can be actively involved, and structure schools where learning is about taking risks and a lifelong venture . . . in which adults believe children will exceed all expectations."

Value creation, the fourth defining feature of personalizable education, means harnessing student skills pertaining to agency, the flexibility within education to innovate, and the communities built by shared ownership of schooling to ensure that what students create has meaning to them and to others and gives them purpose. Meaningfulness is a critical element of learning; we learn about what we care about.

Once again, we are not without models that enable us to move quickly to align inclusive education with personalized learning or personalizable education. MTSS and strengths-based approaches to disability align with principles of personalizable approaches. Promoting self-determination is a critical element in life design and in promoting agency and shared ownership. Another widely adopted practice, universal design for learning (UDL), also provides a framework within which to promote inclusion and personalized education. UDL involves changes to how learning materials and content are presented or represented and how students respond to those materials and content. As Wehmeyer (2019) noted, the principles of UDL align well with the elements of personalizable education:

> . . . providing multiple means of engagement includes tapping into a student's interests and preferences, optimizing student agency, and promoting student self-regulation and self-directed learning;
> . . . . providing for multiple means of representation refers to flexibility in how instructional materials and environments are designed to provide multiple means of content delivery, support understandings of how content interacts and relates and what the big ideas are, and to use multiple ways to present content (e.g., video, audio, digital, print, etc.).
> . . . multiple means of action and expression refers to varying the ways students respond to content, express what they know, and promoting agency through goal setting and attainment. (p. 58)

Inclusive Education Requires Self-Determined Learning

Promoting self-determination has become an important element of the educational programs of most students with disabilities (Wehmeyer & Field, 2007). We discussed the importance of self-determination in Chapter 2 and leave thorough coverage of issues pertaining to self-determination for another volume in the Norton Inclusive Education for Students With Disabilities series. But it is important to emphasize that promoting self-determination is critical to every student, to achieving the goals of a life design approach, to personalized learning, and to inclusive education. As educators, we can enhance student learning by promoting autonomy and choice and by supporting students to engage in activities that are of personal value to them and to act volitionally. If we want to promote student agency and enable students to take ownership over learning, we need to teach them to teach themselves and to learn how to set and achieve goals and make plans. Wehmeyer and Zhao (2020) identify self-determined education as incorporating these elements:

- Teaching starts with the children's passion and talent. Teaching is not to instruct, but to create opportunities for individual students, to help individual students pursue their interest and enhance their abilities, and to help students identify and access resources from within and outside the school.
- Teachers become masterful life coaches who help students identify and achieve personal learning goals, to inspire students to have high aspirations, to explore possibilities, to try out their ambitions, and to learn about their strengths and weaknesses.
- Teachers work collaboratively in a community. They do not teach a group of students in isolated classrooms, but work with individual students as consultants in areas in which they are experts and about which they are passionate.
- Teachers are community organizers and project leaders. Self-determined learning does not mean students always learn alone. Instead very often students learn through authentic projects that involve other students. (p. 68)

Conclusions

A primary purpose of this book is to provide a theoretical and values-driven framework in which to situate the books that will follow in the newly created Norton Inclusive Education for Students With Disabilities series. While this is necessarily a broad-brushed treatment, we hope that it sets out important overall considerations. Put most bluntly, if we continue to do what we have been doing and incrementally include students with disabilities, thousands upon thousands of students will experience an education best characterized by low expectations and segregation that fails to meet the standards set by the U.S. Supreme Court in the *Endrew F.* decision. Further, this is an auspicious time to make significant changes to the education of learners with disabilities because the education of all learners is changing dramatically. As we write these final words, we are six months into the COVID pandemic, an event that has had cataclysmic impact on students, teachers, parents and family members, and education itself. There are clear indicators as to how education, as an enterprise, must change to address inequity and to align with the dramatically changing global learning and economic context. We believe that the "problem" in special education is not the student but a system that at 50 years of age is creaking and has lost relevancy. The 1975 Education for All Handicapped Children Act was a landmark piece of civil rights legislation, but it reflects the knowledge, beliefs, and understandings of its age. Even so, when it was passed almost half a century ago, its framers understood a simple truth: students with disabilities need to be educated with their nondisabled peers in regular education environments.

Inclusive education is not an idea whose time has come. It is an idea whose time came fifty years ago, but for which the field had no model for its implementation. We believe that, with changing ways of understanding disability, alignment with personalized education, and most important, a focus on strengths, inclusive education can become the norm. We believe that teachers have the commitment and skills to move the field in new directions and to support all students.

> *This is an auspicious time to make significant changes to the education of learners with disabilities because the education of all learners is changing dramatically.*

The books in the Inclusive Education for Students With Disabilities series will provide practitioner-oriented guides to designing and implementing appropriately ambitious, inclusive educational practices that benefit all students and that enable learners with disabilities to meet challenging objectives and to succeed in school and life.

Reflective Questions for Group Study

1. Discuss how shifting to a supports paradigm will provide impetus for inclusive and personalized education for all learners.
2. How might a life design approach change how education is structured?
3. What role does promoting self-determination and self-determined learning play in inclusive and personalized education?

References

Abeson, A., & Davis, S. (2000). The parent movement in mental retardation. In M. L. Weh-meyer & J. R. Patton (Eds.), *Mental retardation in the 21st century* (pp. 19–34). ProEd.

Ahlgrim-Delzell, L., Browder, D. M., Wood, L., Stanger, C., Preston, A. I., & Kemp-Inman, A. (2016). Systematic instruction of phonics skills using an iPad for students with developmental disabilities who are AA 5Bach, M. (2017). Changing perspectives on intellectual and developmental disabilities. In M. L. Wehmeyer, I. Brown, M. Percy, K. A. Shogren, & W. L. A. Fung (Eds.), *A comprehensive guide to intellectual and developmental disabilities* (2nd ed., pp. 35–45). Paul H. Brookes.

Ball, D. L., & Forzani, F. M. (2011). Building a common core for learning to teach and con-necting professional learning to practice. *American Educator, 35,* 17–39.

Basham, J. D., Stahl, S., Ortiz, K., Rice, M. F., & Smith, S. (2015). *Equity matters: Digital and online learning for students with disabilities.* Center on Online Learning and Students With Disabilities. http://www.centerononlinelearning.res.ku.edu/equity-matters-digital -and-online-learning-for-students-with-disabilities/

Bauer, K., Iyer, S. N., Boon, R. T., & Fore, C. (2010). Twenty ways for classroom teachers to collaborate with speech-language pathologists. *Intervention in School and Clinic, 45*(5), 333–337.

Blue-Banning, M., Summers, J. A., Frankland, H. C., Louise Lord, N., & Beegle, G. (2004). Dimensions of family and professional partnerships: Constructive guide-lines for collaboration. *Exceptional Children, 70*(2), 167–184. https://doi.org/10 .1177/001440290407000203

Braddock, D., Hemp, R., Rizzolo, M. C., Tanis, E. S., Haffer, L., & Wu, J. (2015). *The state of the states in intellectual and developmental disabilities: Emerging from the great recession* (10th ed.). American Association on Intellectual and Developmental Disabilities.

Browder, D., Spooner, F., Wakeman, S., Trela, K., & Baker, J. N. (2006). Aligning instruc-tion with academic content standards: Finding the link. *Research and Practice for Persons With Severe Disabilities, 31*(4), 309–321. https://doi.org/10.1177/154079690603100404

Buntinx, W. H. E. (2013). Understanding disability: A strengths-based approach.

In M. L. Wehmeyer (Ed.), *Oxford handbook of positive psychology and disability* (pp. 7–18). Oxford University Press.

Burke, M. M., & Goldman, S. E. (2016). Documenting the experiences of special education advocates. *The Journal of Special Education, 51*(1), 3–13. doi:https://doi.org/10.1177/0022466916643714

Caldwell, J. (2011). Disability identify of leaders in the self-advocacy movement. *Intellectual and Developmental Disabilities, 49*(5), 315–326.

Carter, E. W. (2017). The promise and practice of peer support arrangements for students with intellectual and developmental disabilities. *International Review of Research in Developmental Disabilities, 52*, 141–174. doi:https://doi.org/10.1016/bs.irrdd.2017.04.001

Carter, E. W., Austin, D., & Trainor, A. A. (2012). Predictors of postschool employment outcomes for young adults with severe disabilities. *Journal of Disability Policy Studies, 23*(1), 50–63.

Charles, K. J., & Dickens, V. (2012). Closing the communication gap: Web 2.0 tools for enhanced planning and collaboration. *Teaching Exceptional Children, 45*(2), 24–32.

Cole, S. M., Murphy, H. R., Frisby, M. B., Grossi, T. A., & Bolte, H. R. (2020). The relationship of special education placement and student academic outcomes. *The Journal of Special Education.* doi:10.1177/0022466920925033

Cook, S. C., & Rao, K. (2018, 2018/08/01). Systematically applying UDL to effective practices for students with learning disabilities. *Learning Disability Quarterly, 41*(3), 179–191. https://doi.org/10.1177/0731948717749936

Dessemontet, R., & Bless, G. (2013). The impact of including children with intellectual disability in general education classrooms on the academic achievement of their low-, average-, and high-achieving peers. *Journal of Intellectual and Developmental Disability, 38*(1), 23–30.

Dessemontet, R. S., Bless, G., & Morin, D. (2012). Effects of inclusion on the academic achievement and adaptive behaviour of children with intellectual disabilities. *Journal of Intellectual Disability Research, 56*(6), 579–587. https://doi.org/10.1111/j.1365-2788.2011.01497.x

Driedger, D. (1989). *The last civil rights movement: Disabled Peoples' International.* St. Martin's Press.

Erickson, K. A., & Geist, L. A. (2016). The profiles of students with significant cognitive disabilities and complex communication needs. *Augmentative and Alternative Communication, 32*(3), 187–197. https://doi.org/10.1080/07434618.2016.1213312

Every Student Succeeds Act, 20 U.S.C. § 6301 *et seq.* (2015).

Felix, V. G., Mena, L. J., Ostos, R., & Maestre, G. E. (2017). A pilot study of the use of emerging computer technologies to improve the effectiveness of reading and writing therapies in children with Down syndrome. *British Journal of Educational Technology, 48*(2), 611–624.

Finke, E. H., McNaughton, D. B., & Drager, K. D. (2009). "All children can and should have the opportunity to learn": General education teachers' perspectives on including children with autism spectrum disorder who require AAC. *Augmentative and Alternative Communication, 25*(2), 110–122. https://doi.org/10.1080/07434610902886206

Fisher, M., & Meyer, L. H. (2002). Development and social competence after two years for students enrolled in inclusive and self-contained educational programs. *Research and Practice for Persons With Severe Disabilities, 27*(3), 165–174. https://doi.org/10.2511/rpsd.27.3.165

Foreman, P., Arthur-Kelly, M., Pascoe, S., & King, B. S. (2016). Evaluating the educational experiences of students with profound and multiple disabilities in inclusive and segregated classroom settings: An Australian perspective. *Research and Practice for Persons With Severe Disabilities, 29*(3), 183–193. https://doi.org/10.2511/rpsd.29.3.183

Friend, M., Cook, L., Hurley-Chamberlain, D., & Shamberger, C. (2010). Co-teaching: An illustration of the complexity of collaboration in special education. *Journal of Educational and Psychological Consultation, 20*(1), 9–27. https://doi.org/10.1080/10474410903535380

Fuchs, L. S., Fuchs, D., & Compton, D. (2010). Rethinking response to intervention at middle and high school. *School Psychology Review, 39*, 22–28.

Fullan, M., Quinn, J., & McEachen, J. (2018). *Deep learning: Engage the world change the world.* Corwin.

Giangreco, M., & Broer, S. M. (2005). Questionable utilization of paraprofessionals in inclusive schools: Are we addressing symptoms or causes? *Focus on Autism and Other Developmental Disabilities, 20*(1), 10–26.

Giangreco, M., Cloninger, C. J., & Iverson, V. S. (2011). *Choosing Outcomes and Accommodations for Children* (3rd ed.). Paul H. Brookes.

Giangreco, M., Dennis, R., Cloninger, C. J., Edelman, S., & Schattman, R. A. (1993). "I've counted Jon": Transformational experiences of teachers educating students with disabilities. *Exceptional Children, 59*(4), 359–372.

Haines, S. J., Gross, J., Blue-Banning, M., Francis, G. L., & Turnbull, A. (2015). Fostering family-school and community-school partnerships in inclusive schools: Using practice as a guide. *Research and Practice for Persons With Severe Disabilities, 40*(3), 227–239. https://doi.org/10.1177/1540796915594141

Hess, R. S., Molina, A. M., & Kozleski, E. (2006). Until somebody hears me: Parent voice and advocacy in special educational decision making. *British Journal of Special Education, 33*, 148–157.

Horner, R. H., & Sugai, G. (2015). School-wide PBIS: an example of applied behavior analysis implemented at a scale of social importance. *Behavior Analysis in Practice, 8*(1), 80–85.

Hoy, W. (2012). School characteristics that make a difference for the achievement of all students: A 40-year odyssey. *Journal of Educational Administration, 50*(1), 76–97.

Hughes, C., Agran, M., Cosgriff, J. C., & Washington, B. H. (2013). Student self-determination: A preliminary investigation of the role of participation in inclusive settings. *Education and Training in Autism and Developmental Disabilities, 48*(1), 3–17.

Hunt, P., McDonnell, J., & Crockett, M. A. (2012). Reconciling an ecological curricular framework focusing on quality of life outcomes with the development and instruction of standards-based academic goals. *Research and Practice for Persons With Severe Disabilities, 37*(3), 139–152.

Individuals With Disabilities Education Act, 20 U.S.C. § 1400 *et seq.* (2004).

Ioanna, D. (2018). Independent living of individuals with intellectual disability: A combined study of the opinions of parents, educational staff, and individuals with intellectual disability in Greece. *International Journal of Developmental Disabilities, 66*(2), 153–159. https://doi.org/10.1080/20473869.2018.1541560

Jimenez, B. A., & Kamei, A. (2015). Embedded instruction: An evaluation of evidence to inform inclusive practice. *Inclusion, 3*(3), 132–144. https://doi.org/10.1352/2326 -6988-3.3.132

Kalambouka, A., Farrell, A. F., Dyson, A., & Kaplan, I. (2007). The impact of placing pupils with special educational needs in mainstream schools on the achievement of their peers. *Educational Research, 49*(4), 365–382.

Kearns, J., Klienert, H., Harrison, B., Sheppard-Jones, K., Hall, M., & Jones, M. (2010). *What does "college and career ready" mean for students with significant cognitive disabilities?* Lexington, KY: University of Kentucky, National Alternate Assessment Center.

Kennedy, C. H., & Itkonen, T. (2016). Some effects of regular class participation on the social contacts and social networks of high school students with severe disabilities. *Journal of the Association for Persons With Severe Handicaps, 19*(1), 1–10. https://doi.org/10 .1177/154079699401900101

Kleinert, H., Towles-Reeves, E., Quenemoen, R., Thurlow, M., Fluegge, L., Weseman, L., & Kerbel, A. (2015). Where students with the most significant cognitive disabilities are taught. *Exceptional Children, 81*(3), 312–328. https://doi.org/10 .1177/0014402914563697

Kregel, J., & Dean, D. H. (2002). Sheltered vs. supported employment: A direct comparison of long-term earnings outcomes for individuals with cognitive disabilities. In J. Kregel, D.H. Dan, & P. Wehman (Eds.) *Achievements and challenges in employment services for people with disabilities: The longitudinal impact of workplace* (pp. 63–83). Richmond, VA: VCU RRTC. https://vcurrtc.org/resources/viewContent.cfm/151

Kurth, J. A., & Mastergeorge, A. M. (2010). Academic and cognitive profiles of students with autism: Implications for classroom practice and placement. *International Journal of Special Education, 25*(2), 8–14.

Kurth, J., & Mastergeorge, A. M. (2012). Impact of setting and instructional context for adolescents with autism. *Journal of Special Education, 46*(1), 36–48. https://doi.org/10 .1177/0022466910366480

Kurth, J. A., Morningstar, M. E., & Kozleski, E. (2014). The persistence of highly restrictive special education placements for students with low-incidence disabilities. *Research and Practice for Persons with Severe Disabilities, 39*(3), 227–239. doi:https://doi .org/10.1177/1540796914555580

Lance, W. (1976). Who are all the children? *Exceptional Children, 43*, 66–76.

Lee, S. H., Wehmeyer, M. L., Palmer, S. B., Soukup, J. H., & Little, T. D. (2008). Self-determination and access to the general education curriculum. *Journal of Special Education, 42*(2), 91–107.

Longmore, P. (2003). The second phase: From disability rights to disability culture. In P. Longmore (Ed.), *Why I burned by book and other essays on disability* (pp. 214–224). Philadelphia, PA: Temple University Press.

Longmore, P.K., & Umansky, L. (2001). Introduction. Disability history: from the margins to the mainstream. In P.K. Longmore & L. Umansky (Eds.), *The new disability history: American perspectives* (pp. 1–29): New York, NY: New York University Press.

Love, H. R., Zagona, A. L., Kurth, J. A., & Miller, A. L. (2017). Parents' experiences in educational decision making for children and youth with disabilities. *Inclusion, 5*(3), 158–172. https://doi.org/10.1352/2326-6988-5.3.158

Luckasson, R., Borthwick-Duffy, S., Buntix, W. H. E., Coulter, D. L., Craig, E. M., Reeve, A., Schalock, R. L., Snell, M. E., Spitalnik, D. M., Spreat, S., Tassé, M. J., & the American Association on Mental Retardation Ad Hoc Committee on Terminology and Classification. (2002). *Mental retardation: Definition, classification, and systems of supports* (10th ed.). American Association on Mental Retardation.

Lyons, J., Cappadocia, M. C., & Weiss, J. A. (2011). Brief report: Social characteristics of students with autism spectrum disorders across classroom settings. *Journal on Developmental Disabilities, 17*(1), 77–82.

Mazzotti, V. L., Rowe, D. A., Cameto, R., Test, D. W., & Morningstar, M. E. (2013). Identifying and promoting transition evidence-based practices and predictors of success. *Career Development and Transition for Exceptional Individuals, 36*(3), 140–151. https://doi.org/10.1177/2165143413503365

Mazzotti, V. L., Rowe, D. A., Sinclair, J., Poppen, M., Woods, W. E., & Shearer, M. L. (2016). Predictors of post-school success. *Career Development and Transition for Exceptional Individuals, 39*(4), 196–215. https://doi.org/10.1177/2165143415588047

McCart, A. B., Sailor, W. S., Bezdek, J. M., & Satter, A. L. (2014). A framework for inclusive educational delivery systems. *Inclusion, 2*(4), 252–264.

McDonnell, J., Johnson, J. W., & McQuivey, C. (2008). *Embedded instruction for students with developmental disabilities in general education classrooms.* Council for Exceptional Children, Division on Developmental Disabilities.

McDonnell, J., Johnson, J. W., Polychronis, S. C., & Riesen, T. (2002). The effects of embedded instruction on students with moderate disabilities enrolled in general education classes. *Education and Training in Developmental Disabilities, 37*(4), 363–377.

McLeskey, J., Barringer, M.-D., Billingsley, B., Brownell, M., Jackson, D., Kennedy, M., Lewis, T., Maheady, L., Rodriguez, J., Scheller, M. C., Winn, J., & Ziegler, D. (2017). *High-leverage practices in special education.* Council for Exceptional Children and CEEDAR Center. https://ceedar.education.ufl.edu/wp-content/uploads/2017/07/CEC-HLP-Web.pdf

McLeskey, J., Landers, E., Williamson, P., & Hoppey, D. (2012). Are we moving toward educating students with disabilities in less restrictive settings? *Journal of Special Education, 46*(3), 131–140.

McLeskey, J., Waldron, N. L., & Redd, L. (2014). A case study of a highly effective, inclusive elementary school. *Journal of Special Education, 48*(1), 59–70.

Moeyaert, M., Kingbeil, D., Rodabaugh, E., & Turan, M. (2019). Three-level meta-analysis of single-case data regarding the effects of peer tutoring on academic and social-behavioral outcomes for at-risk students and students with disabilities. *Remedial and Special Education.* https://journals.sagepub.com/doi/10.1177/0741932519 855079

Morningstar, M. E., Kurth, J. A., & Johnson, P. J. (2017). Examining national trends in educational placements for students with significant disabilities. *Remedial and Special Education, 38*(1), 3–12. https://doi.org/10.1177/0741932516678327

Morningstar, M. E., Zagona, A. L., Uyanik, H., Xie, J., & Mahal, S. (2017). Implementing college and career readiness: Critical dimensions for youth with severe disabilities. *Research and Practice for Persons With Severe Disabilities, 42*(3), 187–204. https://doi.org/10 .1177/1540796917711439

Murawski, W. W. (2012). Ten tips for using co-planning time more efficiently. *Teaching Exceptional Children, 64*(4), 8–15.

Murphy, M., Redding, S., & Twyman, J. S., eds. (2016). *Personalized learning for states, districts, and schools.* Temple University, Center on Innovations in Learning. https://files.eric .ed.gov/fulltext/ED568173.pdf

National Center for Education Statistics. (2020). *Trends in high school dropout and completion rates in the United States.* Institute of Education Sciences. https://nces.ed.gov/programs/ dropout/ind_03.asp

National Center for Learning Disabilities. (2018). *Agents of their own success: Self-advocacy skills and self-determination for students with disabilities in the era of personalized learning.* https://www .ncld.org/wp-content/uploads/2018/03/Agents-of-Their-Own-Success_Final.pdf

National Education Association. (2016). *Preparing 21st century students for a global society: An educator's guide to the "four Cs."* Author.

Newman, L. (2005). *Family involvement in the educational development of youth with disabilities: A special topic report of findings from the National Longitudinal Transition Study - 2 (NTLS-2).* SRI International.

Newman, L., & Davies-Mercier, E. (2005, Oct.). The school engagement of elementary and middle school students with disabilities. In *Engagement, academics, social adjustment, and independence: The achievements of elementary and middle school students with disabilities.* Special Education Elementary Longitudinal Study. https://www.seels.net/designdocs/ engagement/03_SEELS_outcomes_C3_8-16-04.pdf

Newman, L., Wagner, M., Knokey, A. M., Marder, C., Nagle, K., Shaver, D., & National Center for Special Education Research. (2011). *The post-high school outcomes of young adults with disabilities up to 8 years after high school: A report from the National Longitudinal Transition Study-2.* National Center for Special Education Research.

Office of Disability Employment Policy. (n.d.). *Here's the plan: Your ILP.* U.S. Department of Labor. https://www.dol.gov/agencies/odep/topics/individualized-learning-plan/checklist

Office of Special Education and Rehabilitative Services. (2019). *Forty-first annual report to Congress on the implementation of the Individuals With Disabilities Education Act.* Author.

Orkwis, R., & McLane, K. (1998, Fall). *A curriculum every student can use: Design principles for student access.* ERIC/OSEP Topical Brief. Council for Exceptional Children.

Peck, C. A., Staub, D., Gallucci, C., & Schwartz, I. (2004). Parent perception of the impacts of inclusion on their nondisabled child. *Research and Practice for Persons With Severe Disabilities, 29*(2), 135–143.

Ruijs, N. M., & Peetsma, T. T. (2009). Effects of inclusion on students with and without special educational needs reviewed. *Educational Research Review, 4*(2), 67–79. https://doi.org/10.1016/j.edurev.2009.02.002

Ruppar, A. L., Dymond, S., & Gaffney, J. S. (2011). Teachers' perspectives on literacy instruction for students with severe disabilities who use augmentative and alternative communication. *Research and Practice for Persons with Severe Disabilities, 36*(3–4), 100–112.

Sailor, W., McCart, A. B., & Choi, J. H. (2018). Reconceptualizing inclusive education through multi-tiered systems of support. *Inclusion, 6*(1), 3–18.

Sailor, W., & Roger, B. (2005). Rethinking inclusion: Schoolwide applications. *Phi Delta Kappan, 86*(7), 503–509.

Sannicandro, T., Parish, S. L., Fournier, S., Mitra, M., & Paiewonsky, M. (2018). Employment, income, and SSI effects of postsecondary education for people with intellectual disability. *American Journal of Intellectual and Developmental Disability, 123*(5), 412–425. https://doi.org/10.1352/1944-7558-123.5.412

Savickas, M. L. (2012). Life design: A paradigm for career intervention in the 21st century. *Journal of Counseling and Development, 90*, 13–19.

Savickas, M. L., Nota, L., Rossier, J., Bauwalder, J.-P., Duarte, M. E., Guichard, J., & van Vianen, A. E. M. (2009). Life designing: A paradigm for career construction in the 21st century. *Journal of Vocational Behavior, 75*, 239–250.

Sharma, U., Forlin, C., & Loreman, T. (2008). Impact of training on pre-service teachers' attitudes and concerns about inclusive education and sentiments about persons with disabilities. *Disability and Society, 23*(7), 773–785. https://doi.org/10.1080/09687590802469271

Shogren, K. A., & Wehmeyer, M. L. (2020). Self-determination and transition. In K. A. Shogren & M. L. Wehmeyer (Eds.), *Handbook of adolescent transition education for youth with disabilities* (2nd ed., pp. 195–205). Routledge.

Shogren, K. A., Wehmeyer, M. L., & Lane, K. L. (2016). Embedding interventions to promote self-determination with in multitiered systems of supports. *Exceptionality, 24*(4), 213–224.

Slee, R. (2001). Social justice and the changing directions in educational research: The case of inclusive education. *International Journal of Inclusive Education, 5*(2–3), 167–177.

Smith, D. L., Atmatzidis, K., Capogreco, M., Lloyd-Randolfi, D., & Seman, V. (2017). Evidence-based interventions for increasing work participation for persons with various disabilities. *OTJR: Occupation, Participation and Health, 37*(2 suppl.), 3S–13S. https://doi.org/10.1177/1539449216681276

Smith, J. D., & Wehmeyer, M. L. (2012). *Good blood, bad blood: Science, nature and the myth of the Kallikaks.* American Association on Intellectual and Developmental Disabilities.

Solberg, V.S., Phelps, L.A., Haakenson, K.A., Durham, J.F., & Timmons, J. (2018). The nature and use of individualized learning plans as a promising career intervention strategy. *Journal of Career Development, 39*(6), 500–514.

Sota, M. S. (2016). Co-designing instruction with students. In M. Murphy, S. Redding, & J. S. Twyman (Eds.), *Personalized learning for states, districts, and schools* (pp. 57–71). Temple University, Center on Innovations in Learning. https://files.eric.ed.gov/fulltext/ED568173.pdf

Test, D. W., Mazzotti, V. L., Mustian, A. L., Fowler, C. H., Kortering, L., & Kohler, P. (2009). Evidence-based secondary transition predictors for improving postschool outcomes for students with disabilities. *Career Development for Exceptional Individuals, 32*(3), 160–181. https://doi.org/10.1177/0885728809346960

Thompson, J. R., Bradley, V., Buntinx, W., Schalock, R. L., Shogren, K. A., Snell, M. E., Wehmeyer, M. L., Borthwick-Diffy, S., Coulter, D. L., Craig, E. M., Gomez, S. C., Lachapelle, Y., Luckasson, R. A., Reeve, A., Spreat, S., Tasse, M. J., Verdugo, M., & Yeager, M. H. (2009). Conceptualizing supports and the support needs of people with intellectual disability. *Intellectual and Developmental Disabilities, 47*, 135–146.

Thompson, J. R., Walker, V., Shogren, K. A., & Wehmeyer, M. L. (2018). Expanding inclusive educational opportunities for students with the most significant cognitive disabilities through personalized supports. *Intellectual and Developmental Disabilities, 56*(6), 396–411.

Thompson, J. R., Wehmeyer, M. L., & Hughes, C. (2010). Mind the gap! Implications of person-environment fit models of intellectual disability for students, educators, and schools. *Exceptionality, 18*, 168–181.

Thompson, J. R., Wehmeyer, M. L., Shogren, K. A., & Seo, H. J. (2017). The supports paradigm and intellectual and developmental disabilities. In K. A. Shogren, M. L. Wehmeyer, & N. N. Singh (Eds.), *Handbook of positive psychology in intellectual and developmental disabilities: Translating research into practice* (pp. 23–35). Springer.

Thompson, T. (2016, January 3). The special-education charade: Individualized education programs, or IEPs, are one of the greatest pitfalls of the country's school system. *Atlantic.* https://www.theatlantic.com/education/archive/2016/01/the-charade-of-special-education-programs/421578/

Toews, S. G., Miller, A. L., Kurth, J. A., & Lockman Turner, E. (2020). Unit co-planning for academic and college and career readiness in inclusive secondary classrooms. *Teaching Exceptional Children, 53*(1), 1–8. https://doi.org/10.1177/0040059920916855

Tremblay, P. (2013). Comparative outcomes of two instructional models for students with learning disabilities: Inclusion with co-teaching and solo-taught special education. *Journal of Research in Special Educational Needs, 13*(4), 251–258. https://doi.org/10.1111/j.1471-3802.2012.01270.x

Turnbull, A., Turnbull, H. R., Wehmeyer, M., & Shogren, K. (2019). *Exceptional lives: Practice, progress, and dignity in today's schools* (9th ed.). Pearson.

Turnbull, H. R. (1981). *The least restrictive alternative: Principles and practices.* American Association on Mental Retardation.

Turnbull, H. R. (2019). Foreword. In K. A. Shogren, M. L. Wehmeyer, J. Martinis, & P. Blanck, *Supported decision-making: Theory, research and practice to enhance self-determination and quality of life* (pp. xxi–xxiii). Cambridge University Press.

Turnbull, H. R., Turnbull, A., & Wehmeyer, M. (2010). *Exceptional lives: Special education in today's schools* (6th ed.). Merrill/Prentice Hall.

U.S. Department of Education. (2017). *Issue brief: Personalized learning plans.* Office of Planning, Evaluation and Policy Development. https://www2.ed.gov/rschstat/eval/high-school/personalized-learning-plans.pdf

Watson, S. M. R., Gable, R., & Greenwood, C. R. (2011). Combining ecobehavioral assessment, functional assessment, and response to intervention to promote more effective classroom instruction. *Remedial and Special Education, 32*(4), 334–344.

Weatherly, C. L., & Conrad, M. J. (2016, Apr. 7–9). *Legally defensible programming for students with autism* [Paper presentation]. School Law Seminar, Boston, MA. https://cdn-files.nsba.org/s3fs-public/13-Weatherly-Conrad-Legally-Defensible-Programming-Students-with-Autism-Paper.pdf

Wehman, P., Taylor, J., Brooke, V., Avellone, L., Whittenburg, H., Ham, W., Brooke, A. M., & Carr, S. (2018). Toward competitive employment for persons with intellectual and developmental disabilities: What progress have we made and where do we need to go. *Research and Practice for Persons With Severe Disabilities, 43*(3), 131–144. https://doi.org/10.1177/1540796918777730

Wehmeyer, M. L. (2002). The confluence of person-centered planning and self-determination. In C. S. Holburn & C. Vietz (Eds.), *Person-centered planning: Research, practice, and future directions* (pp. 51–69). Paul H. Brookes.

Wehmeyer, M. L. (2006). Universal design for learning, access to the general education curriculum, and students with mild mental retardation. *Exceptionality, 14,* 225–235.

Wehmeyer, M. L. (2013). *The story of intellectual disability: An evolution of meaning, understanding, and public perception.* Paul H. Brookes.

Wehmeyer, M. L. (2019). *Strengths-based approaches educating all learners with disabilities: Beyond special education.* Teachers College Press.

Wehmeyer, M. L., & Field, S. (2007). *Self-determination: Instructional and assessment strategies.* Corwin Press.

Wehmeyer, M. L., Nota, L., Soresi, S., Shogren, K. A., Morningstar, M., Ferrari, L., Sgaramella, T, & Di Maggio, I. (2019). A crisis in career development: Life designing and implications for transition. *Career Development and Transition for Exceptional Individuals, 42*(3), 179–187.

Wehmeyer, M. L., & Sands, D. J. (Eds.). (1998). *Making it happen: Student involvement in educational planning, decision-making and program implementation.* Paul H. Brookes.

Wehmeyer, M. L., & Ward, M. (1995). The spirit of the IDEA mandate: Student involvement in transition planning. *Journal for Vocational Special Needs Education, 17*, 108–111.

Wehmeyer, M. L., & Webb, K. W. (Eds.). (2012). *Handbook of adolescent transition education for youth with disabilities.* Taylor & Francis.

Wehmeyer, M.L., & Zhao, Y. (2020). *Teaching students to become self-determined learners.* Alexandria, VA: ASCD.

Wei, X., Lenz, K. B., & Blackorby, J. (2012). Math growth trajectories of students with disabilities: Disability category, gender, racial, and socioeconomic status differences from ages 7–17. *Remedial and Special Education, 34*, 154–165. https://doi.org/10.1177/0741932512448253

WHO (World Health Organization). (1980). *International classification of impairments, disabilities, and handicaps. A manual of classification relating to the consequences of disease.* Author.

WHO (World Health Organization). (2001). *International classification of functioning, disability, and health.* Author.

Williams-Diehm, K., Wehmeyer, M. L., Palmer, S., Soukup, J. H., & Garner, N. (2008). Self-determination and student involvement in transition planning: A multivariate analysis. *Journal on Developmental Disabilities, 14*, 25–36.

Wlodarczyk, K. A., Somma, M., Bennett, S., & Gallagher, T. L. (2015). Moving toward inclusion: Inclusion coaches' reflections and discussions in supporting educators in practice. *Exceptionality Education International, 23*(3), 55–73.

Woodman, A. C., Smith, L. E., Greenberg, J. S., & Mailick, M. R. (2016). Contextual factors predict patterns of change in functioning over 10 years among adolescents and adults with autism spectrum disorders. *Journal of Autism and Developmental Disorders, 46*(1), 176–189. https://doi.org/10.1007/s10803-015-2561-z

Yoder, C. L. M., & Cantrell, M. A. (2019). Childhood disability and educational outcomes: A systematic review. *Journal of Pediatric Nursing, 45*, 37–50. https://doi.org/10.1016/j.pedn.2019.01.003

Zhao, Y. (2018). *Reach for greatness: Personalizable education for all children.* Corwin.

Index

About the Authors

Michael L. Wehmeyer, Ph.D., is the Ross and Mariana Beach Distinguished Professor of Special Education; Chair, Department of Special Education; and Director and Senior Scientist, Beach Center on Disability at the University of Kansas. His research focuses on self-determination, positive psychology and disability, and educating students with extensive support needs.

Jennifer A. Kurth is Associate Professor of Special Education at the University of Kansas, and affiliated faculty at the Kansas University Center on Developmental Disabilities (KUCDD) and the Beach Center on Disability at the University of Kansas. Her research centers on inclusive education for students with extensive and pervasive support needs. This includes examining outcomes of inclusion in terms of skill development and quality of life indicators for students with disabilities, as well as how educators develop skills and dispositions for inclusive practices.